IT'S NOT ABOUT THE MONEY

IT'S NOT ABOUT THE MONEY

*A Proven Path to Building Wealth
and Living the Rich Life You Deserve*

SCARLETT COCHRAN, JD

AVERY

an imprint of Penguin Random House

New York

To Joseph, Alexis, and Reeves
for everything

AVERY

an imprint of Penguin Random House LLC
penguinrandomhouse.com

Most Avery books are available at special quantity discounts for bulk purchase
for sales promotions, premiums, fund-raising, and educational needs. Special books
or book excerpts also can be created to fit specific needs. For details, write
SpecialMarkets@penguinrandomhouse.com.

ISBN 9780593421536
eBook ISBN 9780593421543

Printed in the United States of America
1st Printing

Book design by Shannon Nicole Plunkett

Contents

PART 5

CREATE YOUR MONEY PRACTICE — 169

Introduction

It's not about the money . . .

    . . . because you're here to change your life.

Maybe you dream of that white-picket-fence house in the suburbs—or that in-walking-distance-of-everything condo in the city—but you don't know how to get there beyond "save a whole lot of money." Maybe you have big plans to launch your own business and need a firm financial foundation to make the leap. Perhaps you're about to start a family and want to be able to spend on memorable family experiences with your children while they're young, while also building their college funds so that they can attend their dream college like you did. Maybe you're doing well financially but feel there's more you could be doing, if only someone would just sit down and show you the ropes. Maybe you make ends meet every month but are frustrated that your money doesn't go as far as you'd like it to and wish you could retire your credit card and student loan balances faster. Perhaps you just want to feel more confident and in control of your money, knowing that you're on track to build a retirement nest egg that will support your ideal lifestyle in your golden years. Or maybe a global pandemic made you realize that you could lose your job—and your paycheck—at any time. Or you may have a big goal that requires money, like traveling around the world.

Whatever is going on, whatever your big dreams and desires for your life may be, and wherever you're starting out, this book is for you. My mission is to show you that it's possible to live your life the way *you* want to while also being able to meet—or exceed—your financial goals.

Because the truth is that *you* get to choose. Just like no two people are alike, no two lives are exactly alike. Not everyone's financial priorities are, or should be, the same. What you want to spend your money on, what you decide to save for, and what you put first are all individual and completely up to you.

I've spent the last two decades learning every possible thing about how money works, both as a banking and finance attorney and as a single mom struggling to make ends meet, trying to give my child a good life. Today, I help people of all income levels take control of their money and live their best lives *now* while still building wealth for their future. Some of my wisdom is self-taught; I spent many a night in my twenties learning basic concepts like budgeting and how to write a check (remember when those were a thing?). Then I put myself through Yale Law School so I could make more money to support my family. I spent years shaping policy at the Department of Housing and Urban Development, the Federal Deposit Insurance Corporation (FDIC), and the Consumer Financial Protection Bureau (CFPB)—the major federal bank regulators in the United States.

I'm also a single mom who got pregnant at eighteen and had to learn how to manage the little cash I had, fast. Who has been married and divorced and remarried. And who, despite the odds against me, went from living paycheck to paycheck to building a multiple-six-figure nest egg while working a regular nine-to-five public interest job. I have studied or worked in finance for almost twenty years. Long before I'd taken a single law class, I found that I had a knack for intuitively understanding complex financial jargon—a talent that came in handy when a shady mortgage company tried to trick me into an adjustable rate mortgage when I was twenty-two years old. And over the years I've also discovered that I can explain these complex financial topics to other people in a way that makes money feel approachable and even fun—a talent that has helped me to build a successful company, One Big Happy Life, where I've helped millions of people take control of their finances and start using their money to build wealth while creating lives that they absolutely love. And in this book, I'll be sharing these essential keys to holistic wealth building so that you can not only master your money but enjoy it, too.

The first thing I want you to know about this book is that it's going to take a completely different approach to money and building wealth than you've heard before. That's because so much of the conventional wisdom about personal finance is outdated or not grounded in solid financial principles, or is just something someone made up that got repeated enough times that we all started to believe those rules of thumb are the one and only right way to manage money effectively. I know from my own experience and through working with thousands of our members inside Wealth Builders Society that you don't have to follow specific budgeting ratios, be uber frugal, be debt free, or sacrifice your life today in order to be financially secure tomorrow.

The truth is, you don't have to subscribe to anyone else's rules. It's possible to enjoy your life *and* build a future that's fulfilling, flexible, and free. I say often that life is the things that happen between your goals. Small changes that are sustainable—which for most of us does not mean pinching every penny—are what will actually stabilize your finances. And the best part is, you won't have to give up the little and big things that make your days enjoyable.

Trust me when I say: You can find your own answers.

Your own path. Your own way of managing money effictively.

And, like me, you can create a life that you truly love to live while also growing the financial wealth you need to support that life for the rest of your life.

You might already have a mental image of what that life looks like for you. And if you don't, no worries; we'll figure that part out together, too.

I know what it's like to dream of waking up each day feeling excited and energized and in love with the life you've created for yourself. I know what it's like to really, really desire financial freedom, to feel supported and stable. And I know what it's like to dream of moving beyond stability, to want to create real wealth and to leave a legacy for your family or community.

If you're anything like me, it's been a long road already.

Today, I adore my life as a married mom of two and a co-founder (with my partner, Joseph) of One Big Happy Life. But it took me a long time to get here. And I made a lot of mistakes along the way (so you don't have to). My story starts in a small, dingy apartment above a bar when I was just nineteen, living below the poverty line as a single mother-to-be, pregnant with my daughter, Alexis.

I remember one particular morning like it was yesterday. I rolled out of bed and took a few short steps to the bathroom. It was off the hallway, so it didn't have any windows and there wasn't much light.

I hit the light switch and discovered I wasn't alone. We saw each other at the same time, I think, the roach and I, because we both froze. I don't know what it was thinking, but I imagine we shared a similar mix of fear and shock. Yes, I was a Marine who could hit a bull's-eye from five hundred yards away, but yes, I was entirely terrified of a little bug.

Roaches are the worst. Roaches take me back to my childhood, where bugs were a part of everyday life. Where they invaded my precious things no matter how tightly the drawers or cupboards were closed. Where money was so scarce that the response to a roach floating in a glass of orange juice was to fish out the roach and drink it anyway, because orange juice was a luxury and the roaches touched everything anyway. (To be clear, while this orange juice story is true, I was not the one who drank it. Because, roaches. Ew.)

That was a life I had sworn wouldn't be mine again. I'd promised the tiny baby growing in my stomach that it wouldn't be hers, either. Yet there I was, pregnant, facing down another roach. That roach wasn't just a household pest: It was a symbol of everything that was wrong in my life, and of how powerless I felt. I'd tried so hard to eliminate the roaches from my apartment—boric acid, roach baits, I even fumigated the whole place *twice*—and nothing worked. If I couldn't even manage to eliminate the vermin from my apartment, how could I possibly hope to build the amazing life that I envisioned for me and my baby?

I broke the stalemate. I lunged for the roach spray under the sink and gave the bug a taste of floral-scented Raid. Together, we slid to the floor in slow motion, the roach succumbing to the magic of roach spray and me succumbing to just how crappy my life actually was, how far it was from where I wanted it to be, and how impossible it all felt. I was already trying to do my best to manage what little I had. I couldn't afford a nicer apartment because my sub-$25,000 per year active-duty Marine salary would have to pay for day care and diapers and food.

I don't know how long I sat on that bathroom floor, wallowing, sobbing, dreading having to sop up the tiny roach floating in a Raid pool in the corner. But I realized three important truths that day.

First, this was not the life I wanted.

Second, that optimism and wishing were not sound life-planning strategies.

And third?

I needed money.

That morning was life-changing because it began my journey with money. To have more of it in my life. To use what I earned to create the life I wanted.

The more I understood money, the more I came to see it for what it was: an essential tool for creating the life I wanted. By seeing money as a tool, I felt more empowered to learn how to use it effectively. I was excited to learn about how this tool worked and all that it could do for me, whether that was building wealth for my future or buying me my first house and allowing me to travel to new countries. Money was just as essential to my life as food, air, and water. As I grew my money capacity—my ability to use money effectively in every situation—I was able to accomplish everything I'd dreamed of in those early days living in that little apartment, and so much more. After finishing my tour of duty as a Marine, I went on to put myself through college, graduate with my law degree from Yale, and spend ten years as a public interest attorney regulating the banking and consumer finance industries before leaving that career to run One Big Happy Life. Along the way, I built a beautiful life with Alexis, and later with my husband, Joseph, and my son, Reeves.

Twenty years after struggling to buy my first car and figuring out how to pay for college on my own with a family in tow, I was able to pay for my daughter's college education and gift her her first car. I've been able to grow my wealth and financial stability bit by bit, each year's effort building on the last, creating a level of financial comfort that nineteen-year-old me didn't even know to aspire to. And I built up and lived out new dreams—like traveling internationally and becoming a published author—that I never would have believed possible.

You can, too.

Let's start with a major lesson I learned that day (which was not about how to find the most effective, least expensive can of Raid). *Money* was the reason I wasn't living the life I wanted. I could wish and hope for opportunities to come my way, but all the thoughts and Disney princess–style "I want" songs weren't going to pay the deposit on a nicer apartment. If I wanted more out of life, I needed more money. And I needed to be more effective with the money I had so that I was making the most of what I did have. Money touches *everything* we do, from where we live to where we grocery shop to who we hang out with. Every choice we make has financial implications. Just like air, money is always there, whether we think about it or not.

What's unique about money is how much we ignore it. How little we're taught about it. The ways we don't acknowledge it. How we avoid even *mentioning* it. Or how we use coy euphemisms like "I make a good living" or "It was a great value" in order to talk around money instead of saying actual numbers.

If you've ever thought that you're "bad" with money, you're not alone. And it's *definitely* not your fault, because it's very likely no one taught you what to do with it. Most schools don't teach Finance 101, and even if you were lucky enough to get some knowledge from your parents or pick up a thing or two from the internet, it's rarely enough to feel confident about the decisions you're making. And then on top of that, not everything we're taught is true or is good for us. Those well-meaning bits of financial advice and rules of thumb are often errors, inconsistencies, and inaccuracies in the way we talk about money, which can hurt our ability to manage our money effectively.

We're often told what to think instead of being taught the skills we need to help our money work for us. Not to mention that *the way* we're taught about money is often entrenched in shame, fear, and lack. It's not surprising that most people avoid thinking about their money unless they absolutely have to. And when they do think about it or deal with it, the process doesn't feel great. The good news is that money doesn't have to be that way. You can learn how to manage your money effectively and how to enjoy it, too—even in the inevitable moments when things don't go quite as planned and you experience financial setbacks.

Of all the things that matter, that have a day-to-day impact and that directly affect our quality of life, money is probably the most neglected. Studies overwhelmingly show that most of us in the United States are not where we want to be financially. In fact, recent research indicates that 64% of all Americans are living paycheck to paycheck, including 48% of those who make six-figure salaries. More than half of US adults have no emergency savings to cover an unexpected cost of $1,000 or more, and roughly half of those between the ages of fifty-five and sixty-six, with retirement just around the corner, have no personal retirement savings whatsoever. It's no surprise that so many people feel frustrated with their finances.

If you are one of the many, many people who think they are "bad" with money or that they are struggling more than everybody else, let me reassure you that you are not alone. I know from talking with our members inside Wealth Builders Society that *a lot* of them feel that way. In fact, most of us probably feel the way you do. But you're not bad with money. You just haven't been given the opportunity to learn how to create a plan that will work for you. Once you do, you *can* change your life, drastically and surprisingly quickly. Because money is the fuel behind our dreams, our happiness, our fulfillment, and being able to achieve what we want for ourselves.

You've probably heard that money can't buy happiness (which is a total myth, by the way—studies show that spending according to our values does make us happier). While just having money won't automatically solve every problem by itself, it can certainly make life easier—or harder, when you don't have enough of it.

Think about it this way. What do you do when you've had a rough day at work, but there's nothing in the fridge or you just don't want to cook? If you have money, you can order takeout. If you don't, it's a grousing trip to the grocery store or microwaved beans from the back of the cupboard. In addition to allowing you to order pizza when you want it, having money gives you choices. I don't just mean funding a nice vacation, although that's certainly a perk. You can choose to help people you love, or donate to causes that you care about. Money is usually the first thing we need when we are faced with a difficult situation, or even a celebratory moment.

When you shift your perspective to see money not as good or bad but as a tool to build the life you want, it's easier to make decisions that align with your goals. Your dream life and your financial life are intertwined. We can't have one without taking control of the other. When I graduated high school and enlisted as an active-duty US Marine, I didn't see money as something I could control. It seemed to appear like magic in my bank account on the first and fifteenth of every month. The military gave me a roof over my head and food to eat, which meant that I was okay even if I had only fifty cents to my name.

But when I faced solo parenting a baby, I knew that my approach had to change. I had tried to be super frugal—which is how I ended up living in a roach-infested apartment above a noisy bar—but I quickly realized that, with the expenses a little one brings, I *still* didn't have enough. (If you are a parent, you probably recognize this conundrum.) Everything I've been able to accomplish in the past two decades has been with the intention of creating the life I want, and that has usually involved earning more money. I knew that every step I took toward my goals would cost money. I also knew that I wasn't going to do everything overnight, so I strived to make my day-to-day as good as it could be, too.

Now I'm going to help you do the same. I'll show you how it's possible to put your money to work building your future while still being able to enjoy your life today. Like I said, I'm not a big fan of conventional financial advice because it tends to be all or nothing. It tells you that you need to live below your means but never teaches you how to dream bigger for your life and your legacy. It tells you to sacrifice happiness now for happiness later—without acknowledging that you will never. Get. Those. Years. Back. And it teaches you that if you can't or don't want to cut out your daily latte, then *you* are the problem, when the problem is actually the one-size-fits-all generic advice trickled down from the 1980s when pensions were a thing. That approach just doesn't cut it anymore.

You deserve an approach that's balanced and flexible. One that *starts* with what matters to you most instead of leaving it until the end. One that you understand intuitively because you've taken the time to craft it yourself, and one that empowers you to keep learning even as your money—and your life—changes. In this book, I will share how to get there. Because there is a middle ground between financial irresponsibility and worrying over every dime. I live there, and so do the thousands of people who have been through my program, Wealth Builders Society. I'm here to show you how you can enjoy your life today, *and* save for the future, *and* reach financial freedom. *All at the same time.*

I know from my own experience and those of our members in Wealth Builders Society that when we start with an end in mind and know the whys behind our decisions, we're more likely to stick to our plans. That's where my motivation stemmed from. I didn't know everything I wanted that day when I sat crying on my bathroom floor next to a dead roach, but I had an idea, and that spark was enough to propel me forward. I started simple, and so will you.

We're going to start right now, in fact. But I won't ask you to check bank balances or calculate your net worth. Instead, I just want you to think about what you want. What is your first goal?

For me, an early goal was to have $50 in my bank account when the next paycheck arrived. I didn't know what I would do beyond that, and that was okay.

So often, we're afraid to take any path that's not obvious or clear. Whenever I have the opportunity to talk with the members of the

One Big Happy Life community and our Wealth Builders Society members, I hear statements like:

"But what's going to happen if . . . ?"

"How do I know for sure about . . . ?"

"Can you guarantee this is going to work for me?"

My answer to *all* these questions is always the same: Life doesn't come with refunds. There's no way to be 100% sure of anything. So, if you're reading this book with the intent to transform your life and your money—which I assume you are!—then I have your first step right here: Trust yourself to know what's best for you. With the right information and tools at hand, you are more than capable of making financial decisions that will put you solidly on the path to the life you want.

Then I want you to do one more thing.

Believe.

Believe in yourself, in your innate capability, in your enormous potential to make that small step happen. That's what I did. The life I'm living right now started with a simple belief that it was possible for me—even though everyone told me it was impossible. To this day, I still can't tell you exactly what it was that allowed me to believe so strongly in my vision for my future despite having zero support and zero evidence that I could make it happen. But I can tell you that my belief in that future is the thing that drove every action I've taken to get me to this point. Belief is the first step of many to make your dreams come true, even if you can't see the exact path to how from where you're standing right now.

Now, maybe this whole belief thing feels a bit woo-woo to you, given that this is a book about building wealth and managing your money effectively. So I want you to think about it this way: Belief is a precursor for action. Meaning, we only ever take action on things that we believe, on some level, are true. Here's an example of what I mean by that. When I was a kid, I used to be deathly afraid of the toilet monster—you know, the monster that comes out of the toilet at night when you flush it. The only way to be safe from the toilet monster was to make sure you were back in bed and fully under the covers by the time the toilet was done flushing. Then you had to stay covered until the toilet stopped running, a sign that the toilet monster had retreated to his lair. As a child, I spent night after night racing back to bed, worried that the toilet monster would get me. I believed. So hard, in fact, that I suffered many a slammed toe, knee, and hand in the pitch-black race back to bed. Until the day came that I finally stopped believing that the toilet monster was real. The nighttime races ended. A toilet became just a toilet. It's a silly story, to be sure, but it does illustrate the point well. When we believe, we act like the thing we believe in is true. The belief is what keeps us going through the pain of bumping into obstacles and setbacks on the way. The key to changing anything in your life, no matter how small, is first to believe that it's at least possible.

This book isn't just about belief, though. There's real work you'll also need to do in order to build the rich and fulfilling life you want. I'll show you how to dig into that belief and combine it with the numbers so that you can make that dream life your reality.

I'll offer a framework, one you can start with, execute, and tweak as life happens. Because *life* is why you're busting a budget every month, if you're making one at all.

Life is why you dip into savings when the car breaks down, or why your credit card balance is never $0.00. And *life* is why so many people get to their golden years only to find that they didn't set aside enough to be able to retire and afford their ideal lifestyle. The framework I'm going to teach you is made for real life. It's intended to be flexible enough to adapt when it needs to, but still to hold you accountable to actual numbers—numbers that *you* will define based on *your* vision of a deeply fulfilling life.

It puts you in charge of what to spend your money on. I know from experience—my own and those of the millions of people I've had the pleasure of teaching these principles to over the years—that the desire to change our financial lives often comes from a deeper craving for a *different* life. It's not about seeing a number get bigger just for the sake of it. It's about the values we aspire to live out. It's a desire to know that the work we're doing, the way we're making our money, and the way we're spending that money are all creating that fulfilling life we feel called to live.

Money can help us achieve happiness, but let me be clear: Having more money isn't what creates happiness in our lives. It's about the choices we make with our money. And it's easy to fall into bad habits, or to follow the path that other people have laid, not just with our finances but with our thinking, being, and behaving. The genius of the framework I'm offering here is that it will allow you, chapter by chapter, to see what works for your specific situation. The framework you'll put into action puts you in charge. You will learn how to really evaluate your situation, your relationship with money, your habits, and what you're doing to make your life as joyful as it can be.

My story is proof that you can get there. Because if you're anything like me—and the thousands of others who have used this same framework inside Wealth Builders Society—these tools will give you what you need to *finally* feel good about your finances. And *that* is life-changing.

So. Now that you know what you're in for, let's dig in. Pull out a pen and paper, or just consider:

Why do you live the way you do?

Why do you own your house? Rent your apartment? Live with whomever you live with?

Why do you work where you work?

How do you spend your days?

And is that—*any* of that, *all* of that—what you want?

Back when I was just starting out, my goal was to simply feel secure. And to me, counting coupons and worrying about the price of a coffee—well, I knew I wanted a life where I didn't have to do that, where I could buy my lattes and drop things in my grocery cart without having to be vigilant about the price. I'm here to give you permission to feel less stress about whether you're doing the "right" thing with your money, because there *is* no right thing. You can build a seven-figure nest egg without cutting out your daily latte from the cute coffee shop down the street. Or maybe you're a matcha tea kind of person, and you don't feel like you're missing out by making it at home. The choice is up to you.

But you need to shift how you see and use money.

Instead of starting with a budget and a debt-payoff plan, like every other personal finance book ever printed in the history of humankind, you'll start by defining what a good life is for you. What do you want from your life today? In five years? In ten years? Once we have your future mapped, I will help you figure out where you are now. That helps you see the gap between where you are and where you want to go.

Next, I'll demonstrate how the choices you make right now can affect what happens a year from now, five years from now, and when you decide to retire. I'll explain some of the common mistakes people make with their finances, which can seem as innocent as using an emergency fund to replace a busted car tire.

Along the way, I'll provide a framework you can use to secure your financial future—right now and for decades into the future. That's a pretty good ROI (return on investment) for buying this book, if you ask me.

Throughout the book, I'll share exercises that will help you take action and move your financial dreams closer to reality. I suggest dedicating a notebook or a folder on your computer for these exercises so you can start to have all your answers in one place.

Let's get started creating the rich life you deserve.

How to Use This Book

It's Not About the Money is laid out in five parts made up of short chapters, which include exercises, prompts, and step-by-step instructions. I suggest you first read the book from start to finish, completing each chapter's exercises and then moving on to the next chapter. After that, dip in wherever and however is helpful. If you need a refresher on the time value of money, pop back into part 1. If you're feeling that your capacity to spend money comfortably is under strain, revisit part 3 and redo the exercises there. However you revisit this book, *do* revisit it. You are holding a tool and a reference for every stage of your money practice. Remember, it's about progress, not perfection, and I'm here for you every step of the way.

Money Glossary

These are the important terms that will come up over and over as we go. I'll introduce many of them in more detail later, so think of this glossary as a handy cheat sheet to refer back to as you read.

asset—anything you own that either has value and could be sold for cash (such as a house or an investment portfolio) or is held in cash (such as a checking account). The total value of all your assets is your starting point for determining your net worth.

bond—an investment vehicle that allows you to own, and earn money on, part of a loan taken out by a large entity like a company or government. Bonds pay a fixed amount every year, which makes them less volatile than stocks (which can fluctuate either up or down) but also means that the returns tend to be lower. They're also not entirely without risk, as the bond issuer (the entity paying back the loan) might default on the loan (stop paying it back).

budget (*see also* spending plan)—a plan for how you'll spend your money over a given period of time

capacity—a set of skills and mindset shifts that you exercise in one of seven key areas of money management

compound interest—when you earn money from an investment (a return) and that return is added to your principal balance and then also earns interest. Example: $1,000 invested at a 5% monthly rate of return would earn $50 in returns for a total balance at the end of the month of $1,050. In month two, you get a 5% return on both the initial $1,000 and the $50 return from month one, earning $52.50. So at the end of month two, your total balance is $1,102.50. You gained an extra $2.50 in month two because of compound interest.

credit—the ability to borrow money (take on debt)

credit score—a number that lenders use to help determine whether to grant you a line of credit and/or offer you a loan, and what interest rate they should charge you. Your score is affected by things like your amount of existing debt, how long you've had credit lines open, how often you pay on time, and other factors.

debt—money that you borrow from a lender and pay back by an agreed-upon later date, usually with interest

discretionary expenses—expenses that you can spend money on and include in your spending plan but are optional. Example: restaurant meals, salon visits, cable, various subscriptions, and so on.

emergency fund—money set aside for major unexpected financial upheavals, like losing a job or suffering losses in a natural disaster. Usually measured in the number of months of mandatory expenses it could cover. So a three-month emergency fund could keep you fed, clothed, and sheltered for three months without income.

financial freedom number—the amount of money you'll need to sustain your preferred lifestyle when you stop working. The size of your retirement nest egg.

holistic wealth—a concept of wealth beyond acquiring things or money, where each area of your life is at its fullest, richest, deepest, and most meaningful

income—the money you earn from work, or otherwise bring into your life, that is available for you to spend

inflation—the decrease in the purchasing power of money over time

interest/interest rate—interest is the amount a lender charges you to borrow money. Usually expressed as a percentage of the total amount, or the interest rate. You earn interest when you put your money in a savings account or buy a certificate of deposit. In the latter situation, *you're* the lender to the bank, and the bank is rewarding you for the use of your money while it's held in an account at their institution.

investing—putting your money into assets that will grow and/ or produce income over time. This can mean things like buying stocks, bonds, or mutual funds; acquiring real estate to rent out; or buying an ownership interest in a business.

joy—one of the core purposes that money exists to fulfill in our lives

liability—any debt that you own or are responsible for. When calculating your net worth, you subtract the total value of your liabilities from the total value of your assets.

loan—an agreement from a lender to let you borrow a given amount of money according to set terms and conditions

mandatory expenses—also known as fixed expenses, the essential, non-optional things in your life such as food, shelter, utilities, and other basic necessities

minimum investing rate—the amount you must invest each month to reach your financial freedom number by the age you want to retire

money practice—the everyday actions and habits that support and help you achieve your financial and life goals

money rocks—the areas of your spending plan that are most important to you

money stories—the mindsets or ways of thinking that inform how you use money, think of money, and live your life

nest egg—the savings and investments that will provide you with income in retirement. The size your nest egg needs to be is your financial freedom number.

net worth—the total value of all your assets (such as cash, retirement accounts, real estate, valuables, etc.) minus the total value of all your debts and liabilities at any given time

passive income—money you receive that doesn't involve you having to do any work, usually from assets that generate income, such as stocks or bonds that pay dividends. Though many people describe income from side hustles, rental properties, businesses they own, and so on as "passive income," those income streams do not technically fit the definition unless they are truly zero work and hands-off.

portfolio—your collection of income-producing assets and investments. This can refer to all assets of a particular type (such as a real estate portfolio or a stock portfolio) or can be used generally to refer to all such assets.

retirement—the stage of life in which work is no longer your primary source of income

return—the money an investment earns for you, typically expressed as a percentage representing the annual amount of the total investment returned. A $100 investment that grows to $108 in a year has earned you an 8% return.

risk—the likelihood of exposure to negative or unwanted consequences

safety net—a set of resources that can cushion the impact of any unexpected upheavals in your life. This can include emergency funds and sinking funds as well as things like insurance, an estate plan, and a reliable source of passive income.

sinking fund—accounts that you contribute to for a particular purpose. These include things like replacing a major appliance, paying an annual insurance premium, or repairing your roof.

spending plan—a plan you create for how you want to allocate your financial resources based on your goals and values such that following it will move you closer to your dream life while enabling you to live your best life

stability—the ability to withstand or weather downturns or upheavals with minimal negative consequences

stock—an investment vehicle that allows you to own a portion of a publicly traded company (called a share)

stock market—the marketplace where stocks are bought and sold

surplus—the money left over after all necessary expenses have been paid off

time value of money—the principle that the value that money has right now is not the same as it will have in the future. Generally, money is more valuable today than the same amount will be in the future because it can be invested to grow into more money in the future.

wealth (*see also* holistic wealth)—a state of abundance, especially financial abundance, in which resources are sufficient to cover all needs, with surplus left over

PART 1

REDEFINING WEALTH

Chapter 1

WHAT IS MONEY?

When I was a kid, Monopoly was my favorite board game. I loved the thrill of buying new properties, each pass around the board bringing me closer to collecting a matched set. Once I had a full set, I'd upgrade my real estate with little green houses all lined up in a row, only to demolish those houses and replace them with hotels. And I loved collecting the ever-increasing rents whenever someone landed on spaces that I owned.

While playing the game was fun overall, playing with the money was my favorite part. Those slips of colorful paper, each worth more and more. I collected them in neat stacks along my side of the board. I had a thing for the bigger bills, especially the bright orange $500s, which were, of course, the hardest to get. As soon as I had enough money, I'd exchange my smaller bills for bigger denominations at the Monopoly bank. My family found this so exasperating that as soon as I could count well enough, being the banker became my permanent job, which I didn't mind, not one bit. I'd get excited as my orange stack grew and would mourn the loss of each bill whenever I had to break one to pay rent to another player.

Monopoly taught me so many invaluable lessons. That money could help me buy things. That there were things that money could buy that would help me get even more money. That I could strike a deal with someone that would leave both of us happier and wealthier. That I needed to balance spending on new properties with saving reserves in case I needed to pay rent because I landed on someone's property, or if Chance dropped an unexpected bill in my lap. I learned that if you run out of money, it's game over unless you have assets that you can use as collateral for loans. Manage your money wisely and you could get it all back and win.

I also inadvertently learned a few less-than-stellar lessons, like: the person with the most money at the end always wins, and that winning often means having to financially decimate someone else along the way. (Thankfully, those two are not financial facts. Building wealth isn't about racing to be the person who gets the most money the fastest. Also, it's entirely possible to grow your wealth ethically so that everyone can thrive. We'll talk more about how to tell the difference between facts and thoughts in part 2.)

At six years old, I knew very little about money and finance, but I knew enough to know that it was just a game. I knew that whole rainbow of bills was useless to me in the real world. I couldn't take that orange $500 bill to the store to buy real candy, not even the sour apple kind that I loved so much that cost only a penny each. Because Monopoly money wasn't real money. For a long time, all I knew about *real* money was that I needed it to buy things—groceries, movie tickets, cars, clothes.

For something that has such a major impact on our lives, many of us have remarkably little insight into what money is and how it works.

WHY YOU NEED TO UNDERSTAND WHAT MONEY IS

What is money and why is it valuable? Why is it even a thing? Those are the questions we'll be focused on in this section. Even if you think you already know the fundamentals, this section is the scaffolding that all the rest of your understanding about money will be built on. Having a basic understanding of money, the financial system that we live in, and how both have evolved over time will ground your knowledge and make it easier to apply everything that you are going to learn. And it will provide a framework for managing your money effectively in service of your best life even as the financial markets continue to evolve around you.

HOW MONEY BECAME A THING

Humans didn't always have money—at least not how we think of it today. We lived in small communities and relied on social norms of reciprocity and a common understanding of how resources should be shared and distributed. Anything that we weren't able to make or get for ourselves, we would source from our social circles. Within a community, money often took the form of an informal gift economy in which exchanges happened without immediate payment and often without an explicit promise that repayment would ever come.

An exchange in a gift economy looks something like this. Let's say you need a new pair of shoes, but you don't have anything on hand to make yourself a pair. Your neighbor down the street, who has a spare pair, wanders over to your place and offers them to you. You try to tell your neighbor that you have nothing to give them in return. They insist that it's okay because it's a gift. But you both know that you will return the favor in the future should your neighbor need something you have. You thank your neighbor for their generosity and put on your sweet new shoes. The exchange is complete.

Though this type of exchange is often referred to as a gift, if you look closely, you'll see that it resembles another financial instrument that still exists in our society today: debt. Let me buy this thing now and I will pay you later. Yes, the concept of debt is as old as money itself. Some even argue that debt is actually the earliest form of money.*

Bartering was another common form of nonmonetary exchange. Bartering is where you trade goods or services for other goods or services. So again, let's assume you need a pair of shoes. To barter for shoes, you'd need to have some other thing that someone else wants. In this case, let's say that you have several extra bags of grain from your recent harvest. You need to find someone who wants grain right now, and then you'd have to agree on a price. How much grain is a pair of shoes worth? Well, it depends on whom you're asking.

There are several challenges with the barter system. First, it requires a coincidence of wants, meaning that in order for an exchange to happen, you need to find someone who has what you want and *also* wants what you have, which isn't always easy. Second, you can never really be certain of the value of what you have to offer. How much your goods are worth varies depending on whom you are trying to sell to, how badly they want what you have, and how many other people are offering something similar. Third, given how time-consuming and complicated trades are to negotiate, you can only rely on bartering to provide a small amount of what you need to survive.

As societies grew and became more complicated, we started to trade more often, with more people, and with people we didn't know as well, all of which made gift- and barter-based transactions even harder to manage. On top of that, we now had governments that were in charge of protecting us and creating a thriving society, and those governments needed tribute (aka taxes) to sustain themselves and their armies. We needed a way to buy the things we needed from the people who had them. We needed something that both parties valued enough to be willing to make the exchange. We needed money.

---

* David Graeber, *Debt: The First 5,000 Years* (New York: Melville House, 2011).

MONEY CHANGED EVERYTHING

Money evolved as a way to make trade and exchange more efficient. It was a universal store of value all on its own. People understood what a unit of money was worth and that they could use that unit of money to purchase something of value.

Money has evolved over time, with many iterations along the way. Today, we most commonly think of money as paper dollars and coins (even the value of digital currencies like Bitcoin is typically measured in terms of some other physical currency, at least for now). Money has been anything from natural objects like shells, to precious stones and minerals, to paper IOUs redeemable for grain, to modern-day digital currencies that only ever exist in virtual wallets.

Money developed in different ways in different civilizations, but there is one thing that is true across them all: Money is valuable because we agree that it is. Money's sole purpose has only ever been to help us acquire the things we want and its qualities have changed with our needs. Money has changed as our ideas of what money could be have changed.

As money has changed, so have our lives, how we live them, and what we're able to accomplish in them. As money evolved, it made it easier to trade for our wants and needs, both as individuals and as entire societies. We didn't have to rely on knowing someone to trade with them. You could meet Bob for the first time along a road one day, and he'll sell you a pair of shoes in exchange for copper coins because he knows he can immediately use those coins to buy something he needs from someone else. He doesn't have to accept a promise from you that you're good for it at some time in the future.

Money also allowed us to specialize. As transactions became easier to engage in, we didn't have to spend as much of our time meeting our basic needs. A blacksmith could earn money from people who needed horseshoes and tools; then the blacksmith could buy clothes, pans, produce, and supplies.

Money also provided opportunities and freedom. We were no longer tied to a single wealthy landowner who would provide us with food and shelter in exchange for working on their land. We could learn a new trade, move to a new city, be a day worker, and then leave that job for one that paid better.

Finally, as we've become interdependent on others to provide the majority of what we need, money has become more and more important. Even when we are no longer able to work, or just don't want to anymore, we will still need money to provide for ourselves for the rest of our lives.

FINANCIAL SYSTEMS AND THE GLOBAL ECONOMY

We've had a quick history lesson about how money impacts us on an individual and societal level, but that's not the whole story. As money's influence on how we live and work expanded, a new industry sprang up around it: the finance industry. The finance industry arose as a natural result of money becoming more complex and more widely adopted, and as more people realized that money itself provided an opportunity to make more money. Governments play an active part in making, regulating, and redistributing money. We live in a global economy where the events that are happening on one side of the world can have ripple effects on the financial markets and economies of other countries. The movements of the financial markets aren't something we can control or even predict with any real accuracy. The fact that there are some aspects of money and finance that are outside our individual control can cause some people to not want to participate in financial markets because they worry about the risk. But as we'll discuss in depth in the next chapter, participating in financial markets and using them to grow your wealth is an essential part of managing your money effectively. The solution is to understand those markets so that you can make the best possible decisions and put yourself in the best possible position while minimizing risk.

Chapter 2

THE THREE CORE PURPOSES OF MONEY

How you manage your money determines how you live your life. Every life decision is also a financial decision because life costs money. If you want to create the best version of your life, then understanding money and how to use it effectively are nonnegotiable.

Let's talk about purpose—about what money is *for*. Money serves three core purposes: joy, stability, and independence. In part 4, we will take a deeper dive into these three core purposes and how you can use them to guide your financial decision-making, set financial and life goals, and create a money practice that makes managing your finances feel simple and doable.

SPENDING FOR JOY

Joy is what makes life worth living. I want you to understand joy as a core purpose of money, because joy means that you can buy that frothy latte or pick up that fine leather handbag or hire a personal trainer or whatever "living well" means to you. Joy means you can spend quality time with your kids when they're little and watch them thrive at their dream school when they're older. Money brings us joy by making those things possible—by giving us the means to purchase things that make us happy, by opening our world to new experiences, and by letting us relish the value we've created with our work.

CREATING FINANCIAL STABILITY

The second core purpose of money is stability: being protected when the "expected unexpected" happens. Money ensures that if your car gives out, you can still get to work, or if your child breaks her wrist on the playground, you can get her patched up without having to worry about the hospital bill. It's there to cover the expenses that you know will come along but at unpredictable or as-yet-undefined times. In that sense, money is like a seat belt or an airbag: You can't predict if, when, or to what degree you'll need it, but you definitely want it in place when you hit the road.

BUILDING FINANCIAL INDEPENDENCE

The third core purpose of money is to build financial freedom over time. To liberate you from depending on any one job, person, living situation, or other circumstance. Independence means that you always have money flowing in, every month, even if you lose your job or another major source of income, such as your business if you're self-employed.

To achieve true financial freedom, you'll need to build wealth through different kinds of investments, which we'll cover later. This core purpose is a game changer, because once you put the right investment systems in place, money can give you independence all on its own. Even if you're feeling joyful each day and have enough cash to meet your basic needs, if your money isn't building wealth and generating income, you're not tapping into its full potential.

The three core purposes, combined and balanced, are what allow you to build holistic wealth, which is what we'll be talking about next.

Chapter 3

REDEFINING WEALTH

was twenty-three years old when I realized that I could become a millionaire.

After getting my associate's degree from community college, I transferred to Virginia Commonwealth University in the fall of 2005. I'd been accepted to the nursing program, but I changed my major that very first week when I realized that becoming a nurse also meant getting really comfortable with handling bodily fluids. At the time, the only nonmilitary career options I was aware of were doctor/nurse and lawyer. And since that nursing thing clearly wasn't going to work out, the lawyer thing was the only option left. A quick Google search told me that in order to become a lawyer, I'd need to go to law school, and that the best major for a prelaw student was economics. Just like that, I became an economics major.

As an incoming junior with no math or economics background—I didn't even know what economics actually was at that point—intro econ classes dominated my course load. I had room in my schedule for exactly one non-major elective. I scanned the list of available classes, hoping that I'd find one that looked remotely interesting, and I did: Introduction to Personal Finance. My first thought was "Wait—you can just *learn* this stuff in a class?" I'd spent the past five years trying to figure out how to manage my money effectively, learning my lessons the slow and painful way, through experiences and mistakes.

That class fundamentally changed how I thought about money. I showed up on the first day with my brand-new financial calculator ready to soak it all in. My mind was already blown with the realization that personal finance *had its own calculator*.

That class is where I learned the simplest path to becoming a millionaire: small amounts of money consistently invested over a long-enough period of time. You see, there's more to money than its technical dollar amount. Money has the potential to become something *more* in the future. This is called the time value of money, which means that the real value of money today is less than what it could be, because you can invest that money today so that it will grow in the future. Think of money as a seed. You can eat it, you can put it in the pantry for later, or you can plant it and get more seeds. If you pick option C, you can plant those seeds and get even more seeds. That time multiplier that made one seed turn into more and more seeds over time? That's how compound interest and the time value of money work with money.

Let's look at an example using dollars. Let's say that you have $100 and you can invest that $100 at a 5% guaranteed rate of return per year. At the end of year one, you'd have $105 dollars, $5 more than you started with. That 5% return means that $100 today is worth $105 one year from now. If you reinvest that $105 for another year, you'd have $110.25—a whole $10.25 more than you had two years ago. The first year, you made $5. The second year, you made $5.25. That extra twenty-five cents happened because of compounding. And the only thing that you had to do to reap the time value of money was to invest it, then stand back and let the magic happen.

So how do you go from $100 today to $1,000,000 in the future? It depends on four major factors:

1. How much money you're starting with

2. How much money you're going to contribute along the way

3. How long you have to reach the goal

4. The rate of return you expect to receive during that time

The first three factors are largely within your control. You can decide how much money you want to invest toward your long-term wealth and for how long. You can choose where to invest your money, too, but the return will be determined by market forces that you can't control.

If you wanted to become a millionaire in ten years, assuming you're starting from $0 and get 8% average returns over those ten years, you'd need to invest $5,600 per month. Stretch your time horizon out to twenty years, and you'd only need to invest $1,750 per month. Go thirty years out, and your monthly contribution drops down to $700.

Building financial wealth is a matter both of math and of adopting habits that sustain the actions that make the math work. Time is one of the most critical components here. If you have less time, then you will need to put in more money to reach your goal.

Building financial wealth is essential. We all understand the concept of building up a store of resources that we can rely on when we need them. This is the moral of Aesop's fable of the ant and the grasshopper: All summer long, the ant toiled, stockpiling food for the winter. Meanwhile, the grasshopper lounged around, singing his days away. When winter came, the grasshopper had no food. He begged the ant for help, but the ant refused. The story's ending is suspect, but the lesson of planning for the future is a good one. Set aside some of the money that you have today and it will provide for you in the future, as well as create a legacy that outlives you by supporting your descendants and causes that you believe in.

Financial wealth may sound redundant, but I like the term because it makes it clear that there's a broader meaning of *wealth* out there, and many ways you can use money to support your best life. I want you to think of wealth holistically, not as just an accumulation of things or cash, but a way of living a fuller, richer, deeper, and more meaningful life. Which, by the way, is more in line with the ways that we actually use the words *wealth* and *rich*. Those words are not exclusively used to talk about money and finances. For example, a wealth of experience, a wealth of information, a wealth of knowledge. In these examples, *wealth* is used as a synonym for simply having a lot of something, and there is no sense of wealth being excessive or requiring limits. After all, you would never say to someone with a wealth of knowledge that they have *too much* knowledge and should maybe stop building it up. Likewise, a dish can be *rich* in flavor or a food *rich* in nutrients; there's the *rich* sound of an orchestra, or a painting full of *rich* color, or a country with a *rich* cultural history. The point is, when we're defining *wealth* and *richness*, we also need to look at how we use these words, how we think about wealth in other contexts, and apply that mindset to our lives and our finances. When you understand that wealth is not just about financial abundance but about cultivating richness in all aspects of your life, you are empowered with the knowledge that you get to decide what that true abundance should look like. You get to define what makes up your own abundant, infinitely valuable life.

As you read, you will learn how to build holistic wealth, by which I mean wealth that's not constrained or defined by the amount of resources you accumulate but by the quality of your life. Holistic wealth is based on defining your vision of what a rich life looks like for you. It's about using your money to support whatever it is that you most desire. It's about finding the right balance between spending for joy, weaving a safety net, and building financial freedom.

When you commit to building wealth in this way, three amazing things happen. The first is, well, you get to live an incredible life full of wonderful memories and experiences, while also feeling confident in that nest egg that will support you later.

The second perk is that this holistic approach makes it much easier to stick to your wealth plan along the way, because it's based on your *why*. You're not setting financial goals and spending categories based on what someone else says you have to do; you're doing it because you want to. Building wealth to design a life that feels authentic to your unique self is empowering.

Finally, when you set goals from this perspective, from your personal why, you don't have to rely on willpower to make them happen. Willpower is perfectly fine as a tool to psych yourself up before jumping into a cold pool, or to resist that cup of coffee for an hour while you let your whitening strips work, but it is finite—it wears out over time. A longer-lasting and more sustainable form of motivation is the kind that comes from your values, priorities, and sense of self. Intrinsic motivation is in fact the most powerful and renewable source of inspiration we have. You get to fill in the blank.

Action Step

This book has action steps throughout for you to put the principles of each chapter into practice. For a lot of those, you'll be doing some writing, so now is a good time to get a journal or notepad ready. Writing helps you be specific in your thinking, and also gives you a written record of your thoughts that you can revisit later.

Now that you've seen that holistic wealth building is all about articulating that motivation from within, take a moment here to do that. Stop right now, grab a piece of paper, and just write down some thoughts:

- Why does creating a rich and fulfilling life matter to you?

- Why do you want that for yourself?

- What matters to you about that life?

Don't worry too much about what holistic wealth looks like in detail just yet. I'll guide you through specifics in later chapters. For now, the point is just to start building the habit of checking in with yourself, listening to your inner voice, and finding your core motivators. You'll be relying on these to help you make financial decisions that align with your values, and they are what will help you weather the inevitable bumps in the road as you create your rich life.

Chapter 4

CREATING YOUR RICH LIFE

You have big goals and a vision of your best and most fulfilling life. Many people fall short of living the life of their dreams because they don't see a way to make it happen, given their current financial situation. It's hard to change anything if you don't understand how to make it financially possible. The more effective and intentional you are with your money, the better your results will be. The more progress you'll make. The more your life will evolve toward your *best* life, and the more your results will compound.

Building holistic wealth is essential if you want to create the best version of your life, the version of your life that you long for. To do so, you must progress from being "good" with money to being *effective* with money. Traditional financial advice tends to position you as the caretaker of your money, with set rules (and moral judgments) around what makes someone "good" or "bad" with their finances. It's not about what your money can do for you, it's about what you can do with your money. This is backward. Remember, your money's purpose is to serve you, not the other way around.

So let's talk about becoming *effective* with money instead, and how to use it with purpose and vision so it can support you.

GROW YOUR CAPACITY

When we don't understand money, we make choices without full awareness of the available options. The only "bad" financial decision is one where you don't really understand what you're saying yes (or no) to. Being effective with money means being *intentional* with money. It means understanding money so you can exercise that intention, and it means using that understanding to make conscious trade-offs and feel at peace with them.

Being effective with money means that you have mastered—or are working toward mastering—the seven money capacities that we'll cover later in this book. You don't have to be an expert or flawless in your capacities; you just need to feel competent and like you're always learning and improving.

Finally, being effective with money means you are able to manage your thoughts and feelings about the topic so that you can maintain a sense of financial safety and calm even when the inevitable turbulence of life hits.

DEFINE YOUR RICH LIFE

We all want to live meaningful, fulfilling lives. Lives that look and feel exactly the way we want them to. Lives that are filled with memorable experiences with people and places that we love. The way you achieve that life is to first decide that you want it. Then you have to define it, and to commit to it. That vision will be the point of reference from which you make all other financial decisions.

CREATE A MONEY PRACTICE AND BUILD BETTER MONEY HABITS

A money practice is a system for managing your finances that allows you to hit your financial and life goals while spending only as much time as you want on maintaining them. It's helpful to think of the process as a "practice" because that's what you're doing. After all, a *practice* is just the repeated performance of an activity or skill in order to maintain or improve your proficiency. And don't we all want to be more proficient with money, given its impact (as much by its absence as its presence) on our lives? The more proficient we are at something, the easier it becomes and the less energy it takes for us to have extraordinary results.

Let's break it down. The first part of establishing a money practice is applying a system. That can be a big step in and of itself, especially if you're used to last-minute bill paying or avoiding regular check-ins with your finances, but having a system is actually simple. It's just a framework for making decisions and tracking your progress. It's not about blindly following rules or "commonsense" practices so much as committing to a routine and a set of tools. A good system doesn't do the thinking for you, but it streamlines the thinking process so you can channel your money capacities (which we'll describe in part 3) and put them into action. It hits that sweet spot between rigid and haphazard, where it's organized enough to save you time and mental energy but flexible enough to adapt to new strategies as your goals change.

Later, I'll walk you through how to build your own money practice, starting with creating a one-year spending plan. The one-year spending plan (OYSP for short) has helped tens of thousands of people transform their finances because it's adaptable to *you*: Once you understand the setup, you can customize it to suit your needs. Our system is unique, but it does not require you to follow any predefined rules, doesn't dictate anything like savings or debt payoff rates, and doesn't make assumptions about what you want your money to do for you. Make no mistake—the OYSP is comprehensive and life-changing, but it's also easy to execute. You can have yours up and running in just fifteen minutes (more on that in part 5).

The second part of establishing a money practice is calibrating that system so that it allows you to hit your financial and your life goals. Obviously, this means you'll need to know what those goals are—not in a vague "someday I'd like to own a vacation house" sense but at a level of detail that your system can track over time. We'll discuss this when we dive into the minimum investing rate, but that's the basic principle behind this aspect of managing your money: You have both articulated your objectives and know how close or far you are to achieving them. Your system will allow you to see a snapshot of your progress at a given moment, a track record of how you've been doing, and a projection for where you're headed. I want to emphasize *allow* there, because it speaks to the need for balance over rigidity. Managing your money should allow you to both live your best life now and build your dream life for the future. If you're on track to buy a vacation house in five years but you're eating instant ramen for every meal and it's making you miserable, then I would say you're not managing your money effectively. A much better option in that scenario would be to earn more income—whatever it takes to hit that investing goal *and* hit up the gourmet supermarket a few times a week. (Don't worry; we'll get to the how of this, too.)

Finally, if you're managing your money effectively, your system should require only as much time as you want to spend on it. It's not a coincidence that we talk about "spending" time, because time has value, too—arguably much more than money, because we can never earn it back after we've spent it. A healthy, holistic money practice should reflect that value. Some people love a bank statement deep dive and are happy to devote a Saturday afternoon to it every week. Those hours feel totally worth it to them. Others are more set-it-and-forget-it and just want to check in once a month, and that's also fine. Figuring out your best approach will take time to refine, since you have to discover how often you're willing to get hands-on with your finances, but once you understand your rhythm and preferences, you can adjust your system to work the way you want it to.

That's creating a money practice in a nutshell. But there are a few other key points I want to make. First, I believe that *you* are the best person to manage *your* money. Even if you hire an expert to help, like an accountant or a financial planner, you still need to be the director. Those outside people are part of your system and can help nudge you toward your goals, but they're not the ones *setting* the goals. That's all you.

Which brings me to my next point: Anyone can learn to manage their money effectively. Managing money is a skill that you can build with practice and knowledge. There's no barrier to entry other than taking the time to understand how money works, which you're doing right now. It's important to learn how to manage your money, not just because you want to feel comfortable with making financial decisions but also because at the end of the day, no one is going to care about your money more than you. You are the one who has to live with the results of those financial choices, so you don't want to outsource those choices to someone who doesn't have to. This isn't to say you can't outsource some of the systems and busywork, because you can certainly bring in someone else to pull the levers and execute your plan. But before you even consider outsourcing your finances, you want to have that plan in place. You want to have your own money values, goals, and vision for your life straight. Otherwise, you're substituting someone else's values for your own and leaving it up to chance to decide whether that's actually going to create the best outcome for you.

Third, money management is a personal practice. In other words, be wary of giving too much time, attention, or emotional weight to what other people are doing. And certainly, be extra careful about accepting any opinions other people have about what you should be doing. You're working toward your goals, with your system and your values, so don't let anyone else—directly or indirectly—make you feel like you're behind, irresponsible, or otherwise doing it wrong. Expanding your financial knowledge is a lifelong practice, so learning more is always good. But it's important to always view new bits of financial knowledge with a critical eye. If we're not careful, it's all too easy for research to tip us into a shame spiral when we run up against the so-called rules: that you need $X amount saved for retirement by age forty, or that paying over X% in interest is always the wrong move. That's the brilliant thing about building your plan from scratch based on getting where you want to go. If you're ever uncertain about being on the right track, you can check in with your inner compass, and yes, the math.

Effective money management is about what you want, not what anyone tries to tell—or sell—you that you should want. We all want to be able to toss our groceries into our cart without noticing the prices. We all want to live in a space that we love, drive our vehicle of choice, be surrounded by friends and family, and be spontaneous once in a while. We want to have the time to do the things that we're passionate about. We want to do work that's engaging, that challenges us, and that pays us well. And each of us has a unique vision of how all those aspects come together.

So if that unique, personal vision is the project you're building, your personal money practice is like the tool kit. Only you get to choose what's right to get the job done.

PART 2

CHANGE YOUR MONEY STORY

Chapter 5

WHY YOUR MONEY STORY MATTERS

When it comes to the stories we tell ourselves, there's a quote from Henry Ford that I love: "Whether you think you can, or you think you can't, you're right." If you think you can, then you're going to show up as someone who thinks they can. You're going to take actions that align with that belief. If you think you *can't*, you'll show up already defeated. Maybe you won't even show up at all.

In order to show up and take action, you have to, on some level, think that your goal is a possible one. And to turn your thoughts toward possibility, you need to examine the stories that underpin the thoughts that create your default assumptions, your automatic reactions. Our stories are ways of thinking that inform everything we do.

Changing your story allows you to change your thoughts right at the source. We riffle through a *lot* of unconscious thoughts throughout the day—somewhere in the tens of thousands—and that torrent determines what we believe and how we show up. It's critical that we nonjudgmentally recognize the thoughts we are having—especially the ones that aren't bringing us closer to our goals—but if we can recognize the underpinning stories, the patterns of thinking that repeat throughout our days, we can much more efficiently change our trajectory. Consciously shaping your story means that instead of living on autopilot or making knee-jerk decisions, you're making deliberate, intentional choices. And it's deliberate, intentional choices that further our aspirations and make our lives happier.

Everyone has beliefs, scripts, or attitudes that have developed over time: the experiences of growing up with your friends, your family, the community; things that were taught by others and things that you learned through personal experience; something happens, good or bad, and it becomes incorporated into how you see the world. It's all wrapped up together in a mental pattern that influences how you think about everything.

Including, of course, money.

When I was growing up, I wanted to be a writer. But my mom taught me that I should never pursue writing, because writers don't make money. Instead, I should be a doctor or a lawyer.

There's so much to unpack in this one parental lesson. For one, I eventually learned that it wasn't true. But it was the truth as far as my mother knew. She didn't know anyone who had made a living writing. When she thought of financial security, she imagined a few very specific career paths. She was protecting me by giving me the best information that she had so that I could be successful. But she was also limiting me to a box that had nothing to do with me. I did end up becoming a lawyer. I also became a business owner—and, eventually, a writer.

These money stories have so many nuances in your understanding of the world. What's "expensive" versus "cheap." What's okay to spend your money on and what's not. What it means to be "rich" and what it means to be "poor." Whether something is "worth it" or not. And, because money touches every aspect of your life, what you think is *possible*.

The truth is that I didn't learn much about money growing up. I knew I wanted it, because I wanted to be able to buy things the way I saw other people buying things. I knew things cost money, even if I didn't understand how much. I knew I didn't have as much money as other people. I didn't understand anything about how much income would allow for a specific lifestyle. When I got my first job at fourteen working behind the register at McDonald's, my story went from "I want money" to "Ooh, look, I have money!" Every two weeks, I went from no money to new money, and that was amazing. That was pretty much the extent of my comprehension for years to come.

What I did have was a natural tendency to question everything that people told me, especially when what they were telling me was keeping me from what I wanted. I distinctly remember a conversation with my fellow Marines in which I mentioned buying a house. I was nineteen years old. Before I got out the sentence, one of my peers let me know, in no uncertain terms, that there was no way that buying a house would be possible for me.

When I asked them why not, the only answer that they could give me was that it wasn't possible because I was just a lance corporal, a lower level enlisted in the Marine Corps. But when I continued to push and ask what my rank had to do with my ability to buy a house, they couldn't give me a concrete answer.

Everyone seemed to *think* this was true, but no one could say *why*. They just all had this idea that people who were lower in the ranks didn't have what it took to own a house. They assumed that it just wasn't financially possible, period.

So I searched for my own answers, and I discovered that my military rank had nothing to do with whether or not I would be able to qualify for a house. It really came down to the numbers: my income, the amount of the mortgage I was going to take out, and my credit.

That barracks conversation was when I became aware of the money stories that we all internalize. I also realized how much those stories can stand in our way. When we rely on money stories without questioning them, we aren't making our highest and best decisions. We're not making decisions at all, not really. We're living by default.

And no one lives their best life *by default*.

Remember, though, this is not at all your fault. There's no blame to be had. These stories are everywhere—and when I say everywhere, I mean *everywhere*, from casual conversation to parental advice to an episode of *Power Rangers* (stay tuned for that story in a bit). It's no wonder you take them in good faith. Life's busy, you're busy, and most of us never stop to interrogate the rules and the stories about money that we either learned or taught ourselves, especially if those outlooks have been reinforced for decades.

These stories also have an emotional component to them that can be very compelling. For example, many people believe that buying a brand-new car off the lot is a waste of money. But it's just that—a belief. It's a thought, not a fact. And it's a thought that comes from a larger, internalized money story that carries a heavy sense of judgment. No one likes feeling judged, right? So if you hear someone express an opinion based on that story, like the idea that buying a new car is wasteful, it makes perfect sense for your emotional brain to kick in. You don't want to waste money, and you really don't want people to judge you when they see you driving around. You want to avoid those bad feelings. So you convince yourself that this emotionally charged thought is actually a fact. In the end, you don't buy the new car.

But in protecting yourself from the judgment of others, you suppress your own judgment—your own values, wants, and needs. There are plenty of reasons you might value having a new car, and those are completely valid, no matter what conventional wisdom says. These thoughts on what being "good" with money means can actually stop you from using your money to bring you the most benefit. That's why you need to interrogate the "facts" about money that you hear, and think critically about whether there's any truth to them. More often than not, you'll discover that the "facts" you know about money practices are merely thoughts.

Let's go back to the idea that you should never buy a new car because they lose value as soon as you drive them off the lot. Is that a fact or a thought? Well, the second part actually checks out: It is a fact that cars will lose some value after you purchase them, because a used car (no matter how "used" it is) won't be able to sell for as much as a new car. That's just how the market works. But the idea that because of that fact you shouldn't ever buy a new car is just a point of view. That conclusion is based on someone's judgment that the loss in value isn't worth it. But that judgment, like all judgments, is subjective. If you love the latest model electric SUV and you don't want to wait three years for it to start hitting used-car lots, then it's totally worth it to you to buy it fresh from the dealer and get those three years of driving in. If you want to be sure your car has the latest safety features, then it's worth it to buy new and be as up-to-date as possible. Ultimately, it comes down to what you value. (And given that over 66.7 million new cars are sold in the world each year, plenty of people value having a new car.)

This isn't to say that all conventional money wisdom is an erroneous thought or the result of a flawed money story, however. For example, consider the idea that an emergency fund strengthens your financial stability because it helps to protect you from unexpected financial upheaval. Well, that's going to certainly hold true on more occasions than not. At some point in our lives, we will all experience unexpected expenses, whether it's a one-off cost like a speeding ticket or appliance repair or a series of costs due to job loss or illness. An emergency fund is there to help cover those. Sure, it's possible that you could not have an emergency fund and still survive, but the potential risks to your overall well-being would still be really high. And it's also true that an emergency fund could take many forms besides the traditional three-months-of-mandatory-expenses rule of thumb, but certainly having some form of financial resource you can call on in a crisis is better than having none. So we'd file this away as a fact, not a thought. However, while picking apart conventional money wisdom can help you sort out fact from thought on a case-by-case basis, the biggest impact you can have on your decision-making comes from stepping back to look at that bigger money story. That's what this section is all about. Even though these stories can be far-reaching and nearly all-encompassing, they can and do change. Sometimes it happens naturally: You try a food you hated as a kid only to find that, surprise, it's delicious. Others you have to take the initiative to reshape. You have to dig deep, discover what stories you're holding on to, and reexamine them one by one.

I had to change my own story when I decided to apply to law school. I was having a conversation with one of my college professors about which law schools were on my application list. He looked at my list, then turned to me and asked why I wasn't applying to Yale Law. It didn't even occur to me to apply there, because I just assumed I wouldn't get in. I had immigrated to the US when I was two years old. Neither of my parents graduated from high school. I grew up in a hypersegregated inner-city Brooklyn neighborhood where no one went to graduate school, much less an Ivy League school, much less the number one school in the country. So Yale Law had never really seemed possible for me.

But I only realized that I was holding on to this thought, this story, about myself when my professor, a Yale Law alum, asked me what was to him a very obvious question. From his perspective, my not applying to Yale wasn't even an option. He helped me see that Yale was possible for me and was at least worth a shot. And so, with his encouragement, I was able to start shifting a story that was not true. A few days later, I was visiting with my aunt and uncle and I told them that I was thinking of applying to Yale but I had to figure out how to pay for the application. It felt scary to me, wagering $80 on what still felt like a long shot. To my surprise, they believed in me so much that they paid not only for my Yale application but for Harvard and Stanford, too.

My old money story fully shifted, I poured myself into crafting the strongest law school application that I could. I got accepted to all three schools and ultimately decided to go to Yale. Ever since then, I've continued to look for the stories that may be holding me back from that next level of success. I changed my story when I decided to turn down high-paying law firms to go work in the public interest. (Letting go of the story that I had to work crazy hours to make my ideal income.) I changed it when I left practicing law entirely to start my own business. (Letting go of the story that I have to be a lawyer because I paid so much money for the degree.) Every time a story has tempted me to believe that I couldn't achieve something I deeply wanted, I reexamined it and found that the narrative I'd internalized wasn't true.

You'll do lots of that digging and diving in the next few chapters. But a down-and-dirty way to disarm and reframe a story is simply to ask why. In my experience, when I've asked people "Why is that?" in response to some "rule" about money, nine times out of ten, they can't give a solid explanation. They might fall back on "Everyone knows . . ." or just talk around the answer—and that's a clear sign that you can kick that particular belief or approach to the curb.

Looking back, I feel lucky that I grew up with a basically blank slate when it came to money. I didn't know most of our society's typical money stories, so it didn't feel like swimming against the current to work against the ones that were holding me back.

Just to be clear, I'm not telling you to think happy thoughts and you'll manifest wealth tomorrow. Shifting your stories is just the start. You still have to take action, and action takes real effort. But getting your head on straight is the first step *toward* that positive action. After all, if you don't believe it's possible for you to have everything you've ever wanted, why even try?

When you cultivate hopeful, inspiring thoughts and match those with a solid understanding of how money works, the way forward becomes not only simple but doable. From there, the subsequent steps—like creating your spending plan, setting up automatic investments, and everything we'll delve into—are almost effortless. When you go in knowing that something's possible, the pressure to achieve evaporates. You have nothing to prove and everything to gain.

The bottom line is that our stories dictate thoughts, thoughts lead to actions, and actions create wealth.

Action Step

In the chapters of this section, I'm going to walk you through some common money stories that people hold and how to start reframing them. But before we move on, take a moment to write down a list of some of your own money stories.

Grab your journal or notebook and jot down any "facts" about money that come to mind for you. These can be big or small, in any area of your life, work, or identity. Keep those "facts" on hand as you read through the next chapters, and as you encounter typical money stories, reflect on whether your own facts might actually be thoughts based on those stories.

Chapter 6

"BUT I'VE MADE SO MANY BAD MONEY DECISIONS IN THE PAST..."

*E*veryone makes mistakes. We've all heard that from a friend or partner or mentor who's trying to make us feel better in the wake of some regrettable moment. Most people say it as a reflex, whether they're talking to their bestie or their kiddo, telling them "making mistakes is part of life" and "everyone screws up" in a soothing tone of voice. But I want to take a second to consider where this well-meaning story gets us.

My concern is that this framing positions life as a series of mistake after mistake. You don't have to accept that outlook. You don't have to call every choice that you regret a mistake. Give yourself more credit than that. Think about it: When have you ever jumped out of bed and decided to just screw yourself over by doing something really awful? Something you *know* you'll get nothing out of, that will make your life suck afterward, that you'll probably even hate doing *while* you're doing it? Never, right? Because no one does that. No one.

With every choice you make, you're trying to do your best *in the moment*. You're weighing what you value, what you understand, what you feel is right. You're drawing on the experiences you've had up until that point. And so you make the best choices that you can—in that moment. You *don't* go in thinking, "Well, time to make a huge mistake." It's only with time (sometimes a very short time, sometimes weeks or months or years) that you can assign a value judgment to that choice.

And that's where you can get yourself into trouble. Maybe your perspective changes as you experience life, or even just experience the results of that particular choice. You have a new context and fresh eyes to examine it with. You might say to yourself, "I wouldn't do that again." You understand that, knowing what you know now, you'd make a different choice. That's healthy and mature. But too often, we default to "everyone makes mistakes," and from there, it's a slippery slope to "*I* always make mistakes" and "*I* keep screwing up"—it's a fait accompli. Rather than cringing or beating yourself up, it's far more fruitful to try observing yourself and your actions neutrally, or even with gratitude.

Now, as any therapist or mindset coach will tell you, this kind of grounded self-reflection is a good practice in general, but let's bring it back to money. As you saw in the previous chapter, thoughts lead to actions. This is how your blaming yourself over "money mistakes" can easily become a self-fulfilling prophecy. Sometimes, you're taking what you think is positive action, like setting an ambitious goal to "make up" for what you've done, e.g., going from spending your whole paycheck to saving 85% of your income overnight. But because you didn't take the time to really reflect on the choice you made, you're not making this *new* choice in line with your values, either, and you'll find yourself unable to rise to the (impossible) new standards you've set. Then it's time to blame yourself for yet another mistake. Or maybe you'll shrug and stop making choices at all. Those negative feelings are so overwhelming that you'll cop out and just let life happen to you.

Instead of identifying money and how you manage or spend it as a source of shame, you can choose to see it as a place to learn, experiment, and explore. You can recognize that sometimes things that are "bad" will nevertheless serve a purpose that is good for you.

If you find yourself with thoughts like "I'll be paying off this stupid debt for the rest of my life, so what's the point?" or "Well, burned through my paycheck once again with nothing saved—nice going, me," start there. Reflect on what exactly brought you to that choice, the reasons you chose the way you did, and seek out the positive money lesson that you can take from it.

Say you set a budget, and you *really* mean to stick to it this time. But the week goes on, work is hard, your kids won't stop arguing over what show to stream next, and finally one evening you order a take-out feast. You don't say, "Aha, at last, a chance to screw up my own carefully laid plans!" You come home and you're tired. You're hungry. You want to eat. But there's nothing *to* eat. This is a problem. So you pull out your phone and with a few button presses, tacos from your favorite restaurant are making their way to your front door. You solve the problem and use money to do it. You make the best decision that you are able to in that moment, given the circumstances. Looking at it from that perspective, you can understand why you didn't stick to your original spending plan. You can have compassion for yourself, and you can *also* reflect on what brought that problem about. Now, you can put your energy toward finding the patterns that cause your spending to go off track and figuring out how to change them.

It really can be that simple. Being effective with money doesn't mean that you have to be perfect all of the time. It's a learning process that is about trial and error and incremental improvements over the course of your life. I've made plenty of financial decisions over the years that I wouldn't make again if I were faced with the choice today. I call them "wouldn't-do-that-agains." And I'm sure there are plenty of new wouldn't-do-that-agains waiting for me in my future. It's inevitable because life is unpredictable, and as much as we may try to make the best decisions in the moment, all of our decisions won't be winners. And that's okay, because if I made a choice and the result wasn't what I expected—or it *was* what I expected, but it turned out I didn't want it once I had it—that doesn't mean anything about me, my ability to make different financial decisions going forward, or my ability to reach all of my financial goals.

In my second summer of law school, I interned at a law firm that paid me a six-figure salary—more than six times what I'd ever earned at any job up to that point. I decided I was going to treat myself and buy myself a Louis Vuitton bag. So I went to the Louis Vuitton store and I bought this $1,200 bag, which was the most expensive thing I'd ever bought for myself. And I decided that since I'd spent $1,200 on this bag, I was going to wear it all the time, take it everywhere, and use it for everything. I used it in Dallas during my internship, then as my book bag in law school. But after just under a year of carrying my laptop and heavy case books, the strap started to rip off from the bag. When I called Louis Vuitton to ask about a repair, they informed me that a new strap would be $800.

Now, at the time, I was not happy, because how insane is it that this brand doesn't stand by the workmanship of their products? I swore I would never make the mistake of buying a Louis Vuitton bag again. But writing off the purchase as a mistake on my part was just my initial response. Now, further on in life, I don't see it that way at all. I didn't make a mistake. The experience of buying the bag and having the strap rip helped me decide that, no, I will not buy another Louis Vuitton bag until I am in a financial position where I'm fine spending $1,200 on a bag that might need to be replaced within eight months. In fact, I don't want to buy anything that would leave me feeling upset when it breaks and I can't replace it. I also now realize that just because a bag costs a lot does not mean that it's meant to be treated like a heavy-duty utility bag. So many good and practical lessons learned. And now that I know that, I don't need to judge my past self for what happened, because there's no mistake in any of what I did, just lessons learned. Because of that experience I know so much more about myself, my values, and how I like to spend my money.

Having compassion for yourself in the moment and remembering why you made the decisions that you made isn't always easy, but it's important. If you spend your valuable time beating yourself up, then you're missing the lessons. Instead, you can be at peace with how you solved problems in the past, and use what you learned going forward.

- **Old story:** "I'm a failure, I'm so stupid, because I've made so many terrible money decisions."

- **New story:** "I can make better decisions beginning today. All those decisions gave me priceless lessons about what I want, and don't want, and I pledge to *never* repeat them again."

Action Step

Forgive yourself and release your guilt. Pick one particular money moment that makes you feel shame, and remind yourself that you made the best decision you could. Express gratitude for what you learned as a result.

Chapter 7

"BUT I HAVE SO MUCH DEBT . . ."

There is nothing wrong with debt.

Repeat after me: *There is nothing wrong with debt.*

Debt is not something you need to avoid at all costs. Debt is a tool. Debt is useful. Debt is definitely not slavery. And debt is not a reason—or excuse—to put off building wealth.

In my years as a consumer finance attorney and as a wealth coach, I've found that this single fact is the hardest thing for people to wrap their minds around. It's my life's work to keep making the point over and over until the narrative changes.

Most people "know" that debt is bad, a barrier to the life you want. But you know who doesn't think of debt that way? Consumer finance experts. I know this because I spent ten years in consumer finance. My whole job was expanding consumer access to credit—enabling people to use credit and, yes, take on debt. What the experts know, and research backs up, is that access to credit builds stability. Access to credit, when used effectively, allows people to grow their wealth.

When I started teaching about money, I heard how extremely negative the stories about debt were for people: Debt is super burdensome; you're not free until you pay off your mortgage; avoid debt at all costs! My mind was blown. It was clear that a lot of people out there had internalized the polar opposite of what I'd just spent a decade trying to make possible. These stories are pervasive in the conversations around money, and they need to be recontextualized for what they are: debt myths and debt stories. The things I heard from people were statements passed off as facts, but in reality they were just thoughts. And these stories and the thoughts they create cause fear, shame, and anxiety, and stop people from being able to make well-informed decisions about how to use debt in the way that best benefits them, however that may be. That might be having no debt at all, or it might mean carrying various debts over the long term. What matters is that you get to make the decision yourself, without fear and negative emotion.

Debt is just using money to buy time. That's it. So if your time is more valuable to you than your money, then your debt—used smartly and deliberately—can be a benefit. There's no real way to get more time besides buying it, and sometimes you want something now that won't have as much (or any) value to you later on. Debt isn't automatically bad. Rather, the question to ask yourself is whether this debt brings you closer to your goals or not.

Most of us learn to look at debt as an unambiguously negative condition that we have to do away with as soon as possible, because we can't be free without it. We are taught to fear the idea of making payments "for the rest of your life." But there are plenty of things you know you'll be paying for the rest of your life, such as taxes and electric bills. Unless you're going fully off the grid, paying utilities is the cost of the life that you want. Debt is just another lifestyle-supporting cost.

It's important to be cognizant of the stories you're being fed and encouraged to accept, and to think critically about whether or not they are benefiting you. Maybe you're thinking about the fact that you get an ongoing benefit from electricity, that it's useful and it's necessary. Fair enough; let's do the math. Let's say that you pay $70 per month in electricity costs from age twenty-five to age eighty-five—$840 per year over sixty years equals more than $50,000. That's way more than you're spending on those lattes that are supposedly ruining your financial future. Yet you probably don't think of it that way. The fact is, there are other expenses, like this electricity bill, that we expect to pay for the rest of our lives, and it does not cause us anxiety. It's not like the majority of us are constantly wondering where our solar panels are so we can get off the grid and be free of our electric bills, after all. But that electric bill and debt are both expenses. They both contribute to the size of your budget and how much you need to pay out every month. Yet most people choose to look at them differently. They choose to believe that one expense is worse than the other, instead of looking at each of them in terms of the value they bring. We are comfortable knowing the value that electricity provides to our lives, but we don't do that when it comes to debt.

Debt allows you to be able to purchase things now, have them now, and pay for them over time, versus having to wait to buy things until you have the cash in hand. Debt allows you to do things like have a car to drive to work, get an education to kick-start your career, buy a house to raise your family in. When you can't or don't want to wait for something, debt's ability to buy you time provides so much value. For example, when I was pregnant with Alexis, I didn't have anything I needed to take care of the two of us. But I couldn't buy everything I needed with the cash I had, or even the cash I could save over the nine months of my pregnancy. I knew I needed a car, for one thing, but even if I saved up for all nine months, I could maybe put away $2,000 out of my yearly $14,000 salary. Even then, that would have left me driving some old beater, and I wouldn't have had money left to buy any of the other things I needed to make a home for myself and my baby.

So I bought everything on credit. I used debt. My mattress had a payment plan. The first computer that I bought so I could start taking college classes online had a payment plan. If it wasn't for debt, I would have had to put my life off for years, starting my education much later than I did and compromising my child's quality of life. Yes, I paid for the privilege of getting things right at the time I needed them, but it was worth it. That debt enhanced my life. It's what helped me get to where I am right now.

Here's another example. In February 2020, I decided to take my family on an impromptu trip to Disney, partially funded by credit cards. We had drained our travel fund, and we were building it back up that year, but I decided to do this trip then anyway. Kids won't be kids forever, after all. I knew it meant I'd have to pay off my credit cards over the next two months or so, and I was fine planning for that. And then right when we came back, the pandemic happened and we were not able to go on a family trip again for two years. By that time, Alexis was off to college, and those impromptu family vacations were no longer an option. I was already fine using debt to make that vacation happen, but in hindsight, I'm even more glad that I did. Because I chose to rely on debt, we were able to have the joy of the kind of family trip that we would end up unable to take for years of our children's lives afterward.

These examples show why it's so important to be cognizant of the stories you're being fed and encouraged to accept, and to think critically about whether or not those thoughts are actually benefiting you. They show all the value that debt can bring to your life. But to drill down to the core issue here: Yes, you can build wealth while carrying debt. This story means that people either think they can't build wealth *and* pay off debt at the same time, or they know it's possible but assume it's somehow wrong to do so. Neither thought is correct.

We've already touched on how your money can be working toward multiple goals at once. Some can be earmarked toward paying off debt, and some can be earmarked for building wealth. And despite "commonsense" and "rules of thumb" financial advice, there's no reason your plan has to be all one or the other.

When you think about wealth building, you now know that the ultimate goal is financial independence. In order to get there, you have to have sufficient assets (aka wealth) that can provide you with the income you need to cover your expenses when you retire. Paying off debt, on the other hand, reduces your total debt amount and reduces your expenses. But it doesn't put any money toward income-producing assets. In other words, paying off debt docs not in and of itself build wealth.

So paying off debt is one thing and building wealth is another. Your money is capable of working toward multiple financial goals at once. You simply need to plan for both.

The idea that debt reduction should be your number one focus is bad advice because it's overgeneralized. Everyone's priorities and values are different, so everyone should express and manifest those priorities and values in their own way—that just stands to reason. When you don't take your own priorities and values into account before taking action, you're not building a skill set to manage your finances. You're not getting better with money. The one-track focus on debt stops you from exploring and understanding. It stops you from crunching the numbers to figure out which course of action is going to get you to your best outcome. It tells you to make trade-offs but doesn't ask you to weigh your options first—or even present any other options. As a result, you aren't making those trade-offs with intention. You're not making a well-informed choice for your finances.

It's key to point out that, by the same token, paying off debt *could* be the right move. If you sit down, crunch the numbers, and realize that if you spend a year paying off [fill in the blank] dollars, you'll need to put [fill in the blank] more money toward your retirement, but you have a plan to make that a part of your budget and keep yourself on track, then good for you. The problem is that most people *aren't* weighing those options. They've stopped their financial education at "debt bad," and as a result, they're missing out on their wealth-building potential.

This brings me to another issue with this story: It sets up a short-term mindset. If the goal is always to save the most money, you'll spend the minimum possible on a day-to-day basis. You don't consider whether those short-term savings will compromise your longer-term, more expensive and expansive goals. You once again make a trade-off without considering what you've given up. Most of us aren't taught to think long-term, and instead evaluate financial decisions from the perspective of "What will it cost me now?" instead of "What will it cost me now—*and* what it will cost me later?"

Prioritizing debt payoff as the default keeps you from building a critical investment habit. You're not only less likely to invest, but you're also less likely even to seek out information on how to invest. When you add up the years that you haven't been actively investing, it can be difficult to catch up. The investing habit is like a muscle: It takes time and commitment to strengthen, and can diminish without regular practice. The longer you wait to start, the harder it is to pump it up quickly. At the same time, that barbell—aka the nest egg needed for financial freedom—is getting heavier and heavier over time (the time value of money at work).

All that means is that the longer you wait to start investing, the harder you're making it for yourself. By the same token, the sooner you can adjust this story, the better off you'll be. Think of investing as paying yourself first. Future You gets first dibs on the money you bring in, and then it can go to other expenses—including debt. Remember, you haven't made any mistakes here; it can be easy to forget to pay yourself first. As you read on and increase all your money capacities, you'll learn exactly why paying yourself first truly makes sense.

For now, start by reframing debt from something to be ashamed of to a tool for achieving goals in line with your values. Maybe this looks like affirming that you value having a safe new car, and you value it so much that you're willing to take on some debt in order to have it now. Maybe it's that you value your family's health and happiness, so it's worth it to take on debt so that your daughter can get braces and prevent more serious issues down the road.

- **Old story:** "I'll never have financial freedom because I have so much debt."

- **New story:** "I forgive myself for the debt I've accumulated. Debt payments are just another bill, like a phone bill or utility bill. I can pay the bill (no big deal) without any shame."

- **Also:** "I can have debt and build wealth at the same time."

Action Step

Practice gratitude. Why did you take on this debt? What was the benefit to you at the time? What are all the ways this debt has benefited you? Practice savoring this purchase, whatever it is.

Chapter 8

"BUT I LOVE HAVING NICE THINGS..."

G ood news: There's nothing about wealth building that says you can't spend your money on nice things.

When you break wealth building down to its simplest components, there are just two: Spend less than you earn, and invest your money so it will grow over time. Specifically, you have to make sure that you're putting enough away for your wealth to grow at the pace that it needs to support you when it's time to rely on it, so what matters is that gap between earning and spending—the money you'll invest. What doesn't matter is what you spend the money on.

This fact gets lost far too often, so many of us assume that frugality is the only way to wealth, or that there's something morally superior about pinching pennies. Do any of these sound or feel familiar?

- It's not okay to spend money just because you *want* something.

- If you need something, you *have* to spend the least amount possible.

- You should always be on the lookout for bargains and expenses to cut.

But none of those are financial facts. You can purchase nice things and exciting experiences and still build wealth. Look—some people *genuinely love* being thrifty. It feels exciting to them to clip every coupon and watch those numbers tick down at the register. But you do not have to walk a path of frugality if you don't want to. As long as you have that gap between earning and spending, that's all there is to it. Anyone who says otherwise is just projecting *their* values onto *you*. Don't let them.

I remember the exact moment when I decided that I did not want to be frugal. I was attending a finance conference and got invited to a dinner sponsored by a bank. There I was, standing on a balcony overlooking a gorgeous view of trees and a golf course, sipping a habanero cocktail, and, honestly, life felt amazing.

I realized that I wanted to have a life that was filled with those kinds of experiences. Experiences that do cost a lot of money.

Which means I also realized that I needed to create the kind of income that supported my version of a rich life, full of beautiful vistas and as many spicy cocktails as I cared to sip.

If that sounds fabulous to you as well but there's still something holding you back, remember, the financial stories that get in your way are rooted in the thoughts we touched on earlier—those ideas about money that people *present* as facts but are *actually* opinions. Fill in the blank: If you want to build wealth . . . You shouldn't go out to eat. You shouldn't go shopping for fun. You shouldn't lease a car. Actually, you shouldn't have a car payment at all, and if you do, it should be for the oldest, most beat-up, cheapest jalopy you could find because that is all you can realistically afford. There are so many "rules" to frugality, yet they all boil down to it's not okay to spend money on anything but the barest necessities.

By now you know that thought is a fundamentally flawed belief. Money exists to get you what you want. But it's still hard to ignore that little voice saying, *I shouldn't spend on household support when I could do it myself, I have to remember to pack lunch, I need to avoid the mall this week, forget about that fantasy vacation . . .*

Which brings us to your money story: *I feel like I have to choose between what I want and building wealth.*

If you see the path to wealth as nothing but a laundry list of deprivation, well . . . that's probably going to stir up feelings of resentment and resistance to the whole process, which is a surefire way to give up altogether.

But all these feelings are—*say it with me*—just feelings. If you peel them back to the story beneath, you can break out your "But why?" to counter it.

Let's try it. Why does building wealth have to mean saying no to so much?

Or, put another way, what would it look like to have nice things *and* actively build wealth?

I'll tell you one version of what that might look like: earning more income. Which is quite possible—for everyone. For you. You can want and have nice things, and you can build up your wealth for the future, and all you need to do is earn enough to accommodate both goals.

The frugality-or-bust mindset causes blind spots. It diagnoses everyone who isn't cutting their lifestyle to the bone with an overspending problem. But maybe you have an *underearning* problem. Taking control of your financial life means taking a holistic look at your earning and spending habits, and maybe you just . . . don't want to know. You're nervous about what we'll find in there. You're saying, "I can't," but what you mean is "I won't."

That is a completely normal way to feel. But it's also a feeling you can change.

Deep down, you know the truth: If you're spending in a way that doesn't allow you to save, and you want to start, that means you'll have to redirect some of that money to work for you. The problem is that you *like* the way you're spending. You don't want to cut back. I get it.

Here's where the story shift comes in. You've learned that building wealth isn't either/or when it comes to frugality versus luxury. But it's *also* not either/or when it comes to spending versus saving. When you're building wealth, you're not choosing whether to spend or save, you're choosing *when* you're going to spend. You're deciding how much to spend on Present You, and how much to set aside to grow for Future You.

This is why I recommend visualizing your dream life *first*, and then making a spending plan. You get to shop through your imagination, pick out goals from your most abundant dreams, and then make a plan to get there.

To reframe your perspective, start by recognizing what you want for Future You in addition to what you want now. Everything you're doing right now is for the two of you, and you're in control. You get to make the calls. You get to decide what kind of financial resources you want to have available to you when you're ready to stop working.

Of course, not everything is under your control. As time marches on, the future value of your money will get smaller and smaller, so jumping in as early as you can is doing Future You a huge favor. The longer you put it off, the harder and harder, and more and more expensive, it will get over time. (Flip back to page 14 to review the time value of money and the power of compound interest, and you'll see.) It's easy to think you can just get to saving later when your lifestyle slows down, but your dollar is worth more now than it ever will be again, so if you're not saving, the truth is that you're losing money—taking potential wealth out of Future You's hands. There's no better time to start than today to give Future You the best shot at the lifestyle you deserve.

There's one last aspect of this story I want to address before we get to action steps: spending by default. You may not have considered that not all spending is equally satisfying. You're feeling like everything you do, buy, and experience is worth every penny. But what I have found is that when people sit down with the dollars and cents, almost no one is 100% satisfied with where their cash is going. They tell me they don't want to spend that much on lawn care, or wonder why they're paying for a landline they don't even use, or are just plain shocked that the terrible cafeteria bagels they buy at work are costing them two hundred bucks a month.

For me, it came down to eyelashes. I used to get lash extensions done every two weeks and I loved them. I loved them *so* much more than regular strip lashes. I could look myself in the mirror and blink and know that they were a priority. But then the COVID-19 pandemic hit, and I canceled all nonemergency appointments. I realized how much time I had now—to spend with my family, to take my time instead of rushing to the next place or event. I didn't have to be careful about how I slept on my pillow. I didn't have to dance around my eyes while washing my face. It was easier and faster to put on makeup. I didn't feel deprived, either. I felt *relieved*.

The moral of the story is that we all convince ourselves at one point or another that we *must* have things a certain way, but it's not until we test ourselves and go without that we see what we truly need.

- **Old story:** "I'm never going to become wealthy because I like to splurge."

- **New story:** "I can do both."

Action Step

Spend on what brings you the *most* joy. Do you really want another purse, or do you want to go on vacation more? Do you really want to eat out at the same restaurant three times this month, or do you want your future self to have XYZ?

Practice asking yourself: How can I have both? What would that look like? If you truly want both, you can have both—you just need to take the actions to create that reality.

Chapter 9

"BUT MONEY DOESN'T REALLY MATTER, BECAUSE MONEY CAN'T BUY HAPPINESS . . ."

We've all heard "Health over wealth" and "Money can't buy happiness" and "Money is the root of all evil," but until now, you might not have considered that they represent a major mindset block. In reality, there's no either/or, and there's no logical reason to paint money as the enemy of worthwhile objectives like health and happiness. Our culture constantly reinforces this dichotomy, but pushing back on those narratives will lead you to a story of *abundance* instead.

Of course, we've all felt joy and happiness without swiping a credit card; good feelings aren't something you can pick up off the shelf.

But that doesn't mean that money and happiness exist in inverse proportion. Life costs money. Money buys us what we need to survive. Money fixes a lot of problems. Money makes things possible. Money even helps us heal from hurt and trauma by providing access to resources. Money can support you, feed you, protect you, get the health care that you need to save your life, a loved one's life, your pet's life, a stranger's life. Money can't buy happiness, but it can buy support, it can buy experiences, and it can buy *time*—all of which enhance your life.

The other day, my son, Reeves, was watching an episode of *Power Rangers*, and I settled in, too. One Power Ranger was caught in a conflict: She wanted to buy something, but it was expensive. (She said exactly that, over and over again, in a pained tone of voice: "But it's so *expensive*.") I sat up straighter. Right off the bat, the episode was equating expense with unfairness, with *wrongness*, instead of presenting a neutral fact: Things cost what they cost. The main plot then revolved around an evil gym owner who didn't care about other people and was issuing expensive memberships because—as the episode made clear—this gym owner liked money and so was *greedy* and *evil*. The Power Ranger started offering classes for free, so that no one had to pay for the expensive gym, and everyone agreed that, unlike the gym owner, she was a good person.

This Power Ranger was giving away her greatest ability for free because she didn't want to be the same kind of "evil" as the gym owner. (And of *course* it was the girl Power Ranger learning this particular lesson—the wage gap is a massive problem, and now you're teaching young girls that asking for money makes them greedy? That they shouldn't place a value on their time and talents?) There was so much nuance missing. The whole premise of the episode was that she didn't have enough money to do things she wanted to do, and that made her sad, which isn't unreasonable. So why couldn't she find a way to use what she had to earn money, spend that money on what would make her happy, and be generous, not greedy, with others? Why was that kind of win-win option ruled out? She could have done a sliding income scale. She could have done a pay-what-you-can model. She could have done any number of things to earn money, and feel happy, and be generous.

The episode was teaching kids a terrible lesson. Afterward, I did talk with Reeves about it for a bit, but the whole thing got me thinking about how pervasive this story is. Giving things away when you can't even get what *you* want and need? *That's* good and honorable. That's the kind of thing that makes you a hero. Having money? That's not going to make you happy. That's the kind of thing that makes you less likely to be there for others, to have positive values.

This brings me back to the biggest misstep in this story: the idea that "money" and "happiness" are an either/or situation. This is what the writers of the *Power Rangers* episode were doing explicitly, and this is what many people do subconsciously. Yet this logic never seems to apply to other situations. For example, everyone knows that both air *and* water are necessary to keep you alive. But if someone stood up and tried to argue that, *obviously*, water is not necessary for life, because air *is*, or that hydration is the root of all evil, you'd never take them seriously, right? You know that there's no version of the world where they're not *both* essential components for life. You don't attach a value judgment. You just all acknowledge and assume that you need both water and air in order to survive, and so you don't pit them against each other . . . because that would be ridiculous. (Yes, technically, you can survive longer without water than you can without air, but semantics aside, we can all agree that if you never have water, you're still going to die—it's just going to happen more slowly.)

This either/or mentality also paints money as this uniquely evil thing when, in reality, excess of *anything* can be a problem. It doesn't matter if it's money, or sex, or alcohol, or drugs, or sugar, or exercise—even too much water can kill you. Everything in life is that way, because everything requires balance. Used smartly, as a tool, money is a vital resource, an essential component for survival—and something that you need in order to be generous with other people, too.

When we vilify money or its attainment, we're not carving out more space for happiness; we're closing off space for this vital resource in your life. To be good caretakers of our lives, we should also be good caretakers of what makes those lives possible, right? As much as the aphorisms suggest otherwise, money and happiness work hand in hand. When the money-as-villain story is the only story that exists in people's minds, there's no sense of balance, or of possibility. If you feel strongly about your ethics, your money can empower you to live them out, to be a good person on your terms and spread that empowerment to others. Just like the Power Ranger girl could have experimented with ways to earn money and serve others, you can step back from the black-and-white narrative and find your own nuanced options for putting your money to work for your own happiness that's in step with what's most meaningful to you in life.

Let's push back on narratives that perpetuate this stance in our culture, too. Once we can stop categorizing money as immoral, we can start to see it for what it is: a vital tool. Warm up to working with your money instead of fighting it at every turn.

- **Old story:** "Money doesn't matter. Money doesn't buy happiness."

- **New story:** "Money matters . . . a lot! Especially when you don't have enough. That's why it's key to understand it."

Action Step

Write down three things that would genuinely make life feel a little lighter and brighter—for example, "more free time," "clear skin," and "less anxiety." Consider how each (probably) requires money in some way or another and could help you attain them more quickly and with less stress.

Chapter 10

"BUT I CAN'T SAVE FOR THE FUTURE, BECAUSE I BARELY HAVE ENOUGH TO SURVIVE..."

" I struggle with beliefs about what's possible. I worry that the poverty of my upbringing put my financial literacy at a disadvantage. I worry that I'll never be able to achieve financial independence, even though I've earned a PhD in my field and am successful. Sometimes I believe that generations of oppression have put me in a hole that's too deep to dig out of."

This comment came in from a member during a live coaching call inside Wealth Builders Society, and I related to it immediately. I wrestled with this story in law school, where for the first time I encountered multigenerational socioeconomic privilege everywhere I turned. Some of my classmates owned islands, flew first class everywhere, had never struggled financially.

Time and again, I found myself asking why *my* life had to be so hard.

It took me a long time to accept the truth: Their life is their life. My life is my life. There's no point in spending my time wishing for something I could never have. I couldn't magically make my life look like the lives of my classmates. I realized that spending my time focused on other people's advantages wasn't bringing *me* any closer to the life I wanted.

On the other hand, I knew the fact that I had made it that far meant I had many advantages, too. As hard as it had been, there were so many people who, for whatever reason, didn't get the same kinds of opportunities and would look at my life the way I looked at my classmates'.

What I told our members on the coaching call that day, and what I'll tell you now, is that there's always someone who has it better, and there's always someone who has it worse. Focusing on either one, whether it's the guilt of not having it as hard, or the jealousy, frustration, anger, and sense of unfairness over not having the same advantages, isn't productive. Neither one serves you or brings you closer to self-actualization.

What has worked for me is keeping focused on my vision instead. I can't control society's messaging. I can't control who my parents were, what they taught me. I can't change the past to make different choices. All I can control is how I'm going to show up in my life, starting today. I have control over my decisions. I have control over where I put my energy. What I need to think about is not why my life has to be so hard, but what I want my life to look like.

Those are the kinds of questions, the areas of focus, that will bring you closer to the relationship with money that you want to have. Growing up in poverty, going through financial hardships, living hand-to-mouth right now doesn't mean you can't be successful. You absolutely *can*.

Focus on where you are right now. Think about what steps you need to take to create a life that aligns with your vision and your goals. Think about the "next right thing" that you can do to build abundance. If that means saving ten dollars, then start there. If that means saving *five*, then save five. Keep your focus on how *you* are making progress from day to day, week to week, month to month.

If you put your energy into showing up as someone who's on a mission to forge their best life, in every moment and every decision, you will see changes start to happen. Having clarity on your values and objectives will provide you with the motivation that will sustain you through the inevitable obstacles that will come up along the way. You already know you're willing to do the work—you just need to remember that your work will look different from someone else's, and that's okay. It's all *yours*.

An excellent way around this story is to get concrete and specific—as granular as you can—on what you want. So: What do you want, and what are some possible routes that you can take to get there? You'll get a chance to practice this in depth in part 4, but for now, let's focus on where you're starting and where you want to go.

Finally, realize that you've already taken a step forward. You're here, educating yourself, expanding your money capacities, and being intentional with how you spend your time. That's the jumping-off point to demonstrating to yourself that you take your life, your desires, and your ambitions seriously.

- **Old story:** "I can't save and prepare for the future. I am living paycheck to paycheck, and I can barely survive on my current income. There is literally nothing left over to save."

- **New story:** "I save for my future no matter what. I save even during lean times. If I can only save ten dollars a month, then that's what I will do. Ten dollars a month for now. Eventually, twenty. And then, one hundred. And then, more. For me, saving is nonnegotiable."

Action Step

Pick an amount, no matter how small, and commit to saving that much every single pay period. It could be a dollar; it could even be a single penny. In the beginning, it doesn't matter how much you save. It matters more to build a habit of saving. Then start brainstorming what you can do to slowly increase that amount, bit by bit, over time. There's no need to commit to those changes just yet. Just ask yourself the question: If I wanted to increase my savings by X amount next year, what are some ways I could make that happen?

Chapter 11

"BUT IT'S TOO LATE FOR ME, BECAUSE I AM FORTY, FIFTY, SIXTY . . ."

While I was working on this chapter, I traveled to a conference and sat on a Q&A panel with some other money coaches. At one point, someone asked what blocks we have in our businesses or mindsets. Everyone else's were things like concerns over what results they could guarantee and how to package their services. Then it came around to me. I told the audience that the block I have is helping people who are older. That one is hard for me.

I've experienced both money wins and money struggles. I've lived through the ins and outs of investing, buying cars, purchasing property, and building my dream house. I've been through lean times and I've been flush. I've been a single earner and part of a two-income household. But I haven't been in my fifties or sixties or seventies. I don't know what it's like to be older than I am. I can only get there as fast as everyone else does—one year at a time.

But if you're closer to a traditional retirement age, I want you to know that even though I can't directly understand, I do not believe it's ever too late. I don't believe there even is such a thing as "too late." I know that abundance is yours to claim if you choose to. Besides, a "too late" story doesn't add up, because it assumes any of us can *ever* know how much time we have left. "Too late" is simply not a good reason to avoid building your wealth. Yes, you might have fewer years to take advantage of the time value of money, and fewer years to recover from a dip in the market, but you always have choices. There are always decisions that you can make to improve your outcome, no matter your age. You can become more intentional with your spending. You can take the time to establish priorities and values. You can work toward a lifelong dream. You can always take the first step toward the best possible version of your life—*always*.

When you tell yourself it's too late, all your thoughts and actions extend from that story, which shuts down possibility before you even explore what the possibilities *are*. If you resign yourself to your financial struggles, your brain won't go to work to see what you could in fact be doing. You're locked into place, into the exact trajectory that you know with all your heart you *don't* want. Remember: A little better is a little better.

At the same time, the fact that you're saying it's too late . . . tells me that you do have something in mind. There's a second half to that sentence lurking behind the despair: *It's too late for me to afford a vacation to Thailand* or *It's too late for me to build a legacy for my grandchildren*. You know there's something you want, but you're shushing that little voice. What if you instead asked yourself what you can do, what your options are? You can step back from powerlessness into agency just by asking that question and being open to the answer. The point of entry is to recognize that you *do* have options.

Some variables may be set, but you can still work with the other sides of the equation.

For example, consider extending your work life past traditional retirement age. What would it look like if you switched up your industry, your career, your hours? Explore. Everything is in play. Start asking yourself questions. Do you want to take more time and keep working? How could you keep working and make more money? Or find a new field where you really enjoy the work that you're doing? Or both? Being open to possibility allows you to see the options.

Or maybe you can reimagine what retirement will look like for you. After all, there's no reason retirement means quitting the workforce cold turkey, even if you've already retired from one career. If you want to build wealth, this time could be an opportunity to do work you've always wanted to do but never had the chance: because you were busy raising kids, because you'd be starting at entry level, because the job you want is typically part-time or lower paid.

Beyond the building of wealth, which you can begin at any time, there's also the money management side of living a rich life. Things like deciding your financial priorities, reflecting on what brings you joy and meaning, adjusting your spending to be in line with what you value—all those are skills that you're never too old to improve on. In fact, you'll want to practice them each time your priorities and circumstances change. You might realize you're happy to downsize and cut some expenses—or you might realize you don't want to part with anything you own, but get a fresh thrill in revisiting all the things you've brought into your home over the years.

There's also the fact that the more you improve your money skills, the less likely you are to become a victim of something like financial fraud or scams targeting seniors. Sadly, older people are more likely to get taken advantage of, especially if they don't understand how their money works. This doesn't just mean avoiding flat-out scams (the IRS will never ask you to send them gift cards, I guarantee it) but also being skeptical of flashy "once-in-a-lifetime investment opportunities" that market directly to older people with big promises but dubious methods.

Wealth building should always be a holistic process, and when you treat it as a form of values-based decision-making, it's easier to see how to lay a foundation. Look at what matters most to you and then get your money to work to make it happen—however much you have now, however much you want to be earning, and wherever you are in life.

- **Old story:** "It's hopeless. I am already [fill in the blank] years old and I should have started saving and preparing thirty-five years ago. It's too late for me now."

- **New story:** "It is never too late. Even if I'm getting a later start than I would have liked, that's okay. I can always improve my situation."

Action Steps

Consider this moment, right now, as a fresh start. Accept that the past has happened, and release it. Now look toward the future. Given where you are right now, and where you want to be in the future, what's the next action you could take to start shifting your trajectory?

Make a personal win list. List all the things you have going for you: achievements you're proud of, skills you've acquired, memories and moments you're grateful to have lived. Reflect on how the years of your life and the way you chose to spend that time made those wins possible. Then consider how those skills and experiences might serve you going forward.

Chapter 12

"BUT I HAVE A LOW-PAYING PROFESSION . . ."

Maybe this whole time you've been thinking that none of this applies to you because you simply don't earn enough for it to be relevant. First and foremost, let me assure you that you can build wealth on a modest income. You get to define what a rich life looks like for you, remember? In Wealth Builders Society, we have members who are hoping to have multiple homes in different countries, and we have members who want a small homestead living off the grid. We have doctors and we have teachers. We have bankers and we have truck drivers. And the thing they all have in common is that they're all committed to pursuing their unique vision of a rich life and using their money to make it happen. That opportunity is available to you at every income level.

The question then becomes, Is your current profession one you want to stay in? Because, yes, *you have a choice*. How much money you make, who you work for, even your chosen profession, none of that is fixed. You can always decide to walk a different path.

This isn't just wishful thinking, either: Your current salary might *not* be enough to meet your goals and build wealth. But just because that's true right now doesn't mean it has to be true forever. When you recognize you have a choice in how you bring money into your life, and connect more deeply with what you value, you can find ways to bring yourself both fulfillment and financial abundance.

The first step to adjusting this story is to recognize that your current earnings aren't the end of the story. If your job isn't paying you enough, start by asking yourself what job *will* pay what you want, and still allow you to do the kind of work you want to do. What other options are out there?

Yes—there are always other options. It could be a different kind of job altogether, or higher levels and tiers within a career field. Consider different employers in your industry, different positions at your company, different skill sets you could draw upon for a new role entirely, or even simply moving to a different city where pay is higher or the cost of living is lower. Again, the key is not to let the fixed story win and write off those other possibilities without giving yourself the opportunity to consider whether those options are a better fit for you going forward.

I get it—change is scary, and it can feel much easier to stay in the familiar situation where things feel more certain and where you already know the friction points. But know that if you do *want* to change your circumstances, you have the power to do so, to find that job that both pays more and offers rewarding work. You just have to give yourself a little nudge to go from recognizing that a career shift is *theoretically* an option to shaking off your inertia and pursuing it. To do that, you'll likely have to confront the "good reasons" people tend to have for staying exactly where they are right now. They say they're comfortable, and it'd be such a hassle to change, to start a new career or uproot their whole lives to move to a new city. Or that they have a union job and should get pay increases over time if they just wait it out. Maybe they simply know this job and like their co-workers, or they're already settled and that makes life so much easier. They want to live near family, or don't want to move to a lower-cost-of-living area.

All these reasons are valid. In fact, I've used a few of them myself from time to time when it was the most important consideration for me in a particular circumstance. Like the time when Joseph and I committed not to move again until Alexis graduated from high school. I didn't love where we were living at the time, but not disrupting our daughter during those tough teen years was more important to me than anything.

Your reasons for making a decision are yours. The important thing is to recognize that you are making a choice. When we discount our agency in our lives, it leaves us feeling resentful and defeated, like things are happening to us. On the other hand, when we face the reality that we are in fact making a choice to stay in a particular circumstance because it benefits us in some way—now *that* is empowering.

Unfortunately, I see this fixed story—and the resulting burnout—in a lot of people who do public service, nonprofit, or advocacy work, as well as creative types following their passion. In those cases, there's often a hidden second story that tells you that you knew what you were getting into, and this work is too important. You can't put money ahead of what you're doing for others and the world.

For those feeling that way, I see you, and I feel for you. I've done my share of public service work, too, both in the military and in my legal career, and I know how much those kinds of jobs ask of you. But I have to ask you—as I had to ask myself at a certain point—is feeling your resentment build over your low salary in the best interest of the people or cause you want to serve? What would it look like to have your financial goals met *and* feel like your work is making the world a better place? I've seen tons of people make that shift. All you have to do to start is break out of this either/or mentality.

Let's say you're a teacher. Maybe you got into the field because you value access to education. You're conflicted, because you care deeply about the work, but you're burning out fast. It asks a lot of you and doesn't pay enough in return. You aren't living the life you want, and you're stretched too thin to build your legacy. When you started your career, maybe you didn't know what it was *really* like, day to day, to work in a classroom, or you didn't understand what it would feel like to live at that income, and the lean years have started to wear you down. Or maybe the job used to fit with your lifestyle, but your goals have changed, and now there are other things you value, too, like buying a house or starting a family.

Now, you might firmly believe that this job *deserves* higher pay, but you feel like there's nothing you can do other than wait and hope that society comes around. Meanwhile, the idea of leaving your job feels like a betrayal of your value of educational access.

Take a minute to ask yourself: *What would it look like for me to live out my values while still achieving the lifestyle I want and building wealth for the future?*

I'll tell you this much: It won't look like holding out for the pay you "deserve." The problem with this is that you're relying on someone *else* to make it happen. You end up sitting around waiting for society and the market and the law to catch up . . . if it ever does. In the meantime, life passes you by. It's lose-lose—for you, for your fellow teachers, and for your students.

But what it *could* look like is seeking out a better-paying job that still lights you up. When people who are willing and able to leave actually *do* leave, that creates a shortage of supply in that sector, which will push employers to raise wages to attract new employees.

More than that, leaving to pursue a greater income will allow you to dedicate more of your time, energy, and (of course) money into making real change. Maybe you want to be active in the school board or local government to argue for higher pay for teachers. Well, to do that, you need a career and income that gives you the time to show up, do research, and take action. Or maybe you want to get the right people elected to state and federal offices to make more sweeping changes with the stroke of a pen.

You can see how, when you consider the question "What would it look like . . . ?" instead of defaulting to either/or, you can not only achieve that best life now and dream life later, but also make big, values-driven changes far beyond your immediate influence. You can effect change in a lot of ways, but you first have to remember that you have agency, that you have choices, and that making new decisions can still be in step with your values.

The truth is that no one can do everything, all decisions involve trade-offs, and it's up to you to find a balance that works. If you can shift from assuming that abundance and fulfillment are impossible to believing that they are *possible*, then you're already on your way to making new choices. Again, that's not to say that it's going to be easy—growth requires you to stretch—but all you have to do to start is to stretch your story.

And it's not a matter of positive thinking; there are solid financial principles on your side.

First of all, a modest salary isn't in itself a barrier to building wealth. As we've discussed, even small amounts, when invested early and wisely, can build significant wealth over time. There are plenty of people who earn a modest income and still create a plan that allows them to grow millions over the years. If you're not working, it's important that you don't lose sight of the power of the time value of money, and use that to empower your choices. Your smaller investment contributions over thirty years have more growth potential than one or two windfalls over, say, five years. If you've looked at your options and still want to remain where you are, at your current pay grade, you can still build wealth; you'll just have to put together a smart plan to make it happen (we'll get into the nitty-gritty later on).

Second, a fixed mindset presumes that your only means of bringing in money is through your job. In reality, your earning potential is unlimited. You can always find ways to earn more. If you've always wanted to spend your summers traveling, but your public school teacher's salary won't cover the cost of your plane tickets, it's time to brainstorm. We live in a world where it's never been easier to supplement your income with side hustles and investment opportunities. But even your nine-to-five has untapped potential. You could bundle and sell the handouts you make for your classroom on a site like Teachers Pay Teachers. You could tutor on the weekends for standardized test prep. You could teach night courses at a community college. The point is to be open to new and additional solutions.

- **Old story:** "I will never become wealthy because I have a profession that doesn't pay much."

- **New story:** "There are plenty of people who earn a modest annual salary and still manage to build wealth over time. I can set up a smart plan to create $1,000,000 (and more) over the next ten to forty years."

- **Also:** "My earning potential is unlimited. I can find ways to earn more money beyond my paycheck. If my job doesn't provide enough for the lifestyle I want, it's time to start brainstorming what will."

Action Step

Think about whether your current career is still the best career for you, now and over the long term. First, brainstorm what opportunities your current career offers to grow your income over time. Will that growth be enough to support your ideal lifestyle? Next, think about the work itself. Is this the career that you actually want to stay in indefinitely? If you're already feeling some friction in your line of work, maybe now is a good time to look at alternatives and new paths.

Chapter 13

"BUT I AM JUST BAD WITH NUMBERS, PERIOD..."

When I hear "I'm not a numbers person," my response is always, "Of course you aren't, because you never learned it." Very few people are naturally gifted at something they've never formally learned. Once upon a time, you weren't good at walking, either. Or reading. Or writing your name with a pencil. Consider how long it took you to learn those skills: at least a few years, right? And you didn't have to become a virtuoso, either; you mastered the skill to the level you needed it to serve you in your life. Being able to walk doesn't mean you have to train to be an Olympic sprinter. Writing your name successfully doesn't mean you're out here producing hand-lettered calligraphy. But you got to the point where you've practiced for long enough that it all became second nature. You don't even think about it. It's just something you do, a part of who you are.

Managing your money is the same way. It's a skill like any other. If you're worried you can't master it, just give yourself more time and a lower bar.

Now, if you don't especially care for math, that's fine. It's not a deal breaker. Managing money effectively doesn't require you to be a whiz at trigonometry, or even to have your times tables memorized. When it comes to these kinds of numbers, it's less about doing the arithmetic and more about understanding the concepts and principles at work. If you understand percentages, decimals, fractions, and negative numbers, then you have a solid foundation for the concepts we'll cover. You can think of it as the difference between owning a car and being a mechanic. If you're going to own a car, then you need to understand the rules of the road, build your driving skills, get a license, and learn some basic maintenance practices to keep your car in good shape. But no one will demand that you explain how an internal combustion engine works, or insist that you change your own brake pads.

This story is a personal one, and so it tends to be rooted in life experience. If you notice the thought pop into your head that you're bad with numbers, it's going to keep coming back unless you take active steps to counter it.

The first step is awareness. When and where did you get this idea? When was the first time you can remember thinking it? Did someone tell you this—a teacher, a parent? Try to identify that moment. Next, think about when this story comes up now. What situations make you think or feel *I'm bad with numbers*? Do you notice any patterns?

I remember my first time. My family is from South America, and when my mom went to school, she was required to memorize her multiplication and division tables, all the way up to 15. Even as an adult, she could tell you 15 times 14, or 144 divided by 12, or whatever you threw at her, without even thinking. I, however, only learned the times and division tables up to 12. But my mom expected me to learn as much as she had, and by repetition, because that was the way she was taught. But my brain just couldn't do that. The numbers never stuck. I could barely get past 10 without my brain pumping the brakes. It's just simple memorization, but it was so hard for me. In fact, I've never mastered speed multiplication. I still use my fingers to do 9 times tables.

When you're able to identify both the origin of this story and what moments trigger it, then you can start addressing it directly. First, come up with countermeasures for when the thought pops up. One is to ask yourself when the last time you used math to your benefit was. You can also generally think about all the different ways you casually use math day to day.

If you're having trouble thinking of examples, here are some common ones. You know how tall you are, your weight, and how much your weight has changed since you were eighteen. If you have children, you've watched them grow and tracked their progress over time, learned where they fall in percentiles. You know how many years until they're in middle school or high school. If you have a college degree, you kept track of the number of credits you needed to stay on track to graduate. If you need to be at a 10:30 appointment that's a fifteen-minute drive away, then you probably know to be out the door by 10:15. You know that if it's 50 degrees Fahrenheit outside you might need a jacket, and if it's 75 degrees you probably don't. You understand that "buy one, get one free" is the same as getting a 50% discount on those two items. If you're cooking and can't find your one-cup measuring cup, you know you can use two scoops of your ½-cup measure or four scoops of your ¼-cup measure to get the same amount.

Whatever your personal examples, I guarantee you will come up with good ones. You are capable and competent, and you have plenty of evidence to support the fact that you can and do use numbers fluently all the time. Your finances require the exact same kind of understanding. Money management is just more of the same: knowing what $500 will buy in groceries and whether or not you want to spend that much, weighing the higher salary of a new job versus the cost of a longer commute, benchmarking whether 6% is a reasonable annual return on an investment, given the level of risk involved. Doing this exercise, and telling your brain that you are capable of handling numbers and have the evidence to prove it, counteracts this counterproductive story.

This was the case for me not just when it came to personal money management, but also in my professional life. I grew up thinking that I was *just not great with numbers* because my brain does not allow me to maintain my 15 times tables the way my mom's did. But what I eventually came to realize is that you don't have to be able to master these numerical skills when you have aids and tools to help. So, even though I wasn't a whiz at mental double-digit multiplication, I was still good enough to be on the math team by the time I hit seventh grade. I understood the concepts and the principles, which ended up being more important to the big picture.

Furthermore, I was also good enough to be a banking and finance attorney many years later. I had to understand the numbers, of course, but not as deeply as the economists and statisticians that I worked with. I didn't need that same depth of knowledge about all the statistics, how they were calculated, and how the analysts crunched the data. I didn't need to know any of that in order to be successful at my job, and I don't need to know it now to manage my finances.

The things you need to know, you can learn. But you don't have to know everything, so you don't have to learn everything, either. It's about figuring out how you can learn the concepts and execute them in a way that works for you. If you have 9 times 8 down cold, great. If you still need to use your fingers, also great. If you need a calculator or an abacus or whatever—great, because that doesn't matter. We use whatever tools we need to do this work. Unlike what your middle school algebra teacher may have told you, you *can* have a calculator in the real world, whenever you want, among many other useful tools.

What matters isn't whether you're "good" with numbers, but whether you care about your wealth and want to feel empowered about money. If you have that desire to learn to manage your money with confidence and feel good about your financial decisions and the life that you're building dollar by dollar, then that's all you need. That desire is enough for you to figure out a way to make the financial side work for you and your brain.

In part 3, I'll discuss the seven money capacities: how each appears in your life, what a lack of that capacity entails, and how it affects you. I'll explain what your life might look like if you master each one, and then how you can continue to hone that skill. Strengthening your capacities is a continuous process. It's a practice, not a one-and-done deal. You can always revisit and refresh, and there will *not* be a pop quiz.

- **Old story:** "I'm just bad with money. I'm an artist! I'm not a numbers person! This isn't my strength and never will be."

- **New story:** "I can learn how to manage money and do it effectively. This is a must-have skill, not an optional skill. I have learned new skills before and I can learn this, too."

Action Step

Think back to the first time you can recall feeling like you were "not a numbers person." What person or event triggered that feeling in you? How can you view that moment differently now?

Reflect on another time when you felt like you were bad with numbers and what triggered that thought in you. Then come up with counterarguments based on all the ways you use numbers and numerical reasoning in your daily life. How do you feel?

PART 3

EXPAND YOUR MONEY CAPACITY

Chapter 14

THE SEVEN MONEY CAPACITIES

Being effective with money isn't a fixed or inborn trait. It's a set of skills that you can acquire, build up, and improve on. Anyone can learn them. You can learn them. This section will teach you how.

When we talk about being effective with money, we're talking about seven key areas of capacity. These capacities represent all the ways of interacting with money that everyone should get used to recognizing and navigating. They are: understand, decide, earn, have, spend, lose, grow. All together, they comprise your financial fluency.

These capacities are the skills that are essential, yet they may not be the ones that first come to mind. When you think of what it takes to manage your money, you might think of the hard skills: budgeting, crunching numbers, paying bills, those sorts of things. You might not consider more abstract thinking, judgments, and values. But these "soft" skills are just as essential. They're what help you feel competent in managing your finances and making your money do what you want it to do.

More than that, these capacities expand your sense of what your money can do. They help you see its full potential and power. Focusing on adding up numbers and balancing checkbooks lends money only a limited sphere of influence, as something that lives in a spreadsheet or a bank portal. It's only about the pool of dollars and cents in your possession right now. This short-term focus stops you from being able to fully lean into a future-focused view of your finances—where you actually have the most potential for changing your financial trajectory. The full picture requires knowing how and when money enters your life, and growing that input as needed. It's about using all seven of these capacities.

As you read on, you might find you're fairly strong and confident when it comes to certain capacities, and less confident with others. Maybe you're pretty good at earn and spend, but you have less experience with lose and grow. That's normal. Everyone draws on their own experiences with money. All that matters is that you stretch yourself and grow all the capacities, not just your innate strengths. Think of it like becoming a five-star chef. You need to enjoy food. You should understand flavors, textures, and a wide variety of cuisines. But you also need to learn certain underlying principles. You need to know the difference between baking and roasting, and between poaching and boiling, and the safe temperature to cook pork to versus beef. You need to practice using your hands, learn how to use a knife, how to flip an omelet, how to knead dough. All these abilities come together when you prepare and serve that beautiful plate of food.

Similarly, if you don't use your capacities consistently, they might fade over time. In that sense, it's like brushing your teeth. If you don't brush for ten years, you can't make up for it by brushing for a full hour before you see the dentist. You're still going to need a root canal. But taking five minutes twice a day will keep you cavity-free. A consistent practice also naturally keeps you up-to-date. Your life and the financial world will alter over time, but your capacities can grow and adapt with you.

At the end of the day, it's not just about learning how to be better at something. It's about building your sense of what's possible and bringing it into sharp focus. It's taking yourself from a fixed mindset to a growth mindset and understanding that you *can* expand your capacity in all seven areas over time. It's about knowing yourself and trusting yourself.

Let's get started.

Chapter 15

UNDERSTANDING

First things first. You need to *understand* money—what it is, what it can do for you, how it works. This capacity is the prerequisite for all that follows. You don't need to know everything on earth, but you need to know the basics. You need a vocabulary so you can sit down with a loan officer or financial planner and know what kinds of questions to ask.

The first two parts of this book already got you started on building this capacity. This is a big, critical first step. Thinking about money and always learning more can and should be a normal part of life, because every decision we make is a financial one.

Understanding money is a lifelong learning experience. This capacity is one that you'll never stop growing, not just because your own situation will evolve but because the world will change, too. Understanding starts with basics like what it takes for an average person to manage their money (which we've already talked about), and how and why the financial landscape and system around us shifts and adapts.

It's easy to think of the pillars of our Western financial system, like credit scores, the stock market, and annual tax returns, as just the way things are or even the way things always have been. In reality, these systems can and do evolve, recalibrate, or even fade away, sometimes incrementally, and sometimes drastically over a short period of time.

Take the stock market, for example. Before the stock market came about, the only way a person could make money from a company was to found one or own one. The idea that an average person could buy a tiny portion of ownership of that company—a stock—was revolutionary. You didn't need to be related to J. P. Morgan to profit off the US Steel Corporation; you could just buy stock in the company. When the company's value goes up, the price of the stock increases, and you make money by selling your share to someone else at that new, higher price. It sounds basic enough to us now, but at the advent of the stock market, the capacity to understand this huge shift was not something to take for granted, and a lack of that understanding could lead to unintended losses. But the nature of the market continued to evolve. With the introduction of mutual funds in 1924, you could now own partial shares of many different stocks. This spread out your risk in a way that hadn't been possible before, a real benefit. But there was more to understand about mutual funds than this novel perk. Because a person in the investment firm had to be responsible for managing these funds, the firms charged you more to invest in them, to offset the employment cost—not to mention that a manager controlling the contents of the fund brought the potential for human error as they would speculate (aka gamble) on which asset mix would provide the best return.

Understanding how these funds worked, and how their benefits and downsides stacked up to those of single-company stocks, suddenly became very important for ordinary investors. Yes, mutual funds were new and innovative, but unless you understood how they worked, you couldn't know for sure whether they were the right choice for you to invest in. You needed the capacity to understand. The same was true at the introduction of yet another kind of fund, the exchange-traded fund, or ETF, in 1993. ETFs are similar to mutual funds in that they are bundles of stocks and bonds, but they are passively managed, not actively managed, so they tend to have lower fees. And with even more recent stock-investing options you can buy fractional shares of individual stocks. The financial markets and the financial products within them continue to evolve, with each new iteration requiring investors to put their capacity for understanding to work.

The need for this capacity isn't limited to understanding changes in the stock market. The vehicles for spending, saving, investing, and earning money evolve faster than you may realize. For example, the 401(k), one of the most common and familiar retirement investment accounts here in the US, feels like it has always been around but in fact only just came about in the 1970s. Mortgage disclosures and the financial regulations governing them changed significantly after the 2008 financial crisis. The Tax Cuts and Jobs Act of 2017 made some of the most dramatic changes to how Americans are taxed and credited on their annual returns in over thirty years. And fintech (financial technology) start-ups are popping up right and left with everything from debit cards that let you get your paycheck three days earlier to peer-to-peer money transfer apps.

The point is that the world of money is continuously evolving, and that's what makes the capacity to understand so vital. It's not about memorizing the rules and regulations of what's out there right now; it's about having the skills and confidence to investigate, to learn, and not to assume things will always be as they are now. When you understand money, you can examine the pros and cons and make a decision for yourself. Maybe that new get-paid-sooner debit card sounds like a great idea. But maybe the deposits aren't FDIC-insured.

Understanding what that actually means—namely, if the company folds, you aren't guaranteed to get your money back—could be a big factor in whether you sign up or not.

Specific examples aside, all you need to understand is that these things can—and will—change throughout your life. It's important to find a comfortable balance in your understanding, too. You want to continue to be well informed, but you aren't going down rabbit holes on everything finance related (unless that's your jam). You can make choices as new products and options emerge. Learn their ins and outs, or become just familiar enough with them to make the decision about whether you want to participate. This way, you're neither confused nor locked into old strategies that might become obsolete over time.

Understanding doesn't mean simply having your basic facts and principles down. It means you grasp what you're doing *before* you spend or promise to spend any of your money. It means you feel confident that you can fill in the gaps in your knowledge with a little effort. Remember, the only "bad" financial decision is one where you don't fully understand what you're saying yes to, and that's why this capacity is so key. You should never enter into a transaction that you don't understand. When you take it as a given that understanding is a capacity you can exercise, and a prerequisite to getting involved in any financial activity, you will feel empowered to ask as many questions as you need before you sign on the dotted line.

Our emotions can hold us back from exercising this capacity to its fullest. Maybe you don't like confrontation, maybe you don't want to look dumb, maybe you feel embarrassed that you don't understand the contract in front of you. You have to let those feelings go. Even when you have a baseline of working knowledge, so many financial transactions are unique. As a result, it's impossible for nearly anyone to understand every term at first glance.

True understanding means feeling comfortable asking questions and getting a thorough grasp on the terms you're presented with.

In action, this capacity might look like a conversation with a loan officer. Instead of a five-minute meeting during which you present your ID and documents and then sign your name and get out of there (perhaps because you don't want to seem like you don't know what you're doing), you go in confident in what you do *and* don't know, and you make your need for knowledge clear from the get-go. Tell them you want to make sure that you completely understand the terms of this transaction, and that it's really important to you that the loan officer takes the time to go through it line by line. Notice that you're not even asking a question; you're stating up front that the two of you *will* be reviewing everything. Your loan officer says of course, they're happy to help, so you dive in with as many specific questions as you have: what the terms mean, what the individual numbers are, whether the interest rate can change, what the late-payment fees are, or even just what a particular clause actually means in plain English. Trust me, they will not be fazed. With every question, listen to what the loan officer says and then decide if you understand the answer, or if something doesn't seem right, you ask them again and rephrase it in your own words. If you get the sense that they're saying something out loud that doesn't totally correspond with what the agreement says, you thank them for explaining and ask them to put their spoken explanation in writing.

At that point, your loan officer makes any changes, you shake on it and get everything signed and done with. That's the ideal scenario, anyway. Understanding also means that you're willing to walk away if anything doesn't feel right or doesn't add up. Understanding means you are confident in the fact that anyone offering you a transaction that's on the up-and-up, that's meant to be mutually beneficial and not trying to take advantage, will be willing to be patient and answer your questions. And it also means knowing your rights as a person, a consumer, a mortgagee, or whatever role you assume in a given transaction.

This goes beyond what we tend to think of as financial transactions, too. Understanding doesn't just come into play in that loan officer's office, or when you're signing up for a credit card or negotiating a payment plan; it's also critical when you hit someone's car, when you fill out onboarding paperwork at a new job, when you decide to start training for a marathon. Those are all transactions in one way or another. You're constantly engaging in all sorts of contracts with legal and financial ramifications, and at the end of the day, you're the one who's going to have to deal with whatever comes from them.

You are the one who has to live with the outcome, so make sure you always understand what you're getting into. Avoid making decisions in the present that have unwanted consequences in the long term. The better you understand money, the easier it is for you to manage it and to make decisions that are more likely to have the outcome you want.

Action Steps

Go back and reread an earlier section of the book that still feels confusing. Read it again until you fully understand the lessons.

Practice asking questions about a financial transaction, either one you've already completed or one you're considering.

Chapter 16

DECIDING

The second money capacity is *deciding*. You need to know how to make decisions about money, and you need a system for making those decisions. As I've said, *every* decision we make is a financial decision, because money is almost always involved. But it's never only about comparing numbers. It's about knowing what you care about and value. When you decide with intention and forethought, you go beyond figuring out which option gets you the bigger (or smaller) number in the end. You consider the options and possibilities and trade-offs involved, and choose the one that aligns with the life you want.

Years ago, I was trying to figure out where I should go to law school. I had to make a difficult (but extremely fortunate) decision between Yale, Harvard, Stanford, or a full-ride scholarship to the University of Michigan. That's a difference of real numbers—we're talking hundreds of thousands of dollars. But I knew that law school wasn't just a one-and-done purchase; it represented the next three years of my life and an education to launch my career. I thought about what my life would be like with each choice. How would it change? What would it be like to live in Connecticut versus California? What would my expenses be when I finished law school? How would I pay back six figures' worth of student loans if I decided not to take the scholarship?

In the end, my decision was part number crunching and part forward thinking. That's how I approach a big decision. I considered the trade-offs between cost and life experience.

Developing your capacity to decide is all about uncovering what you want and all the ways you could get there, and choosing the path that feels most appealing. It may be appealing because it's the fastest. It may be appealing because it's the most efficient, or requires the least sacrifices, or just feel the most fun. No matter what, you want to pick your path thoughtfully, rather than hastily. When you're comfortable in your capacity to decide, you understand that you don't have to wait for life to happen to you. You can plan your finances in advance and figure out how much money you will need for each fork in the road, and you are open to possibilities instead of pre-rejecting any potential option.

The first step is to simply decide what you want. (We'll do more of this in chapter 24.) For instance, maybe you're considering where to live, and you decide you want a three-bedroom house with a view of the lake.

Then, consider all the possibilities that might get you there. What are the different ways you could live in that three-bedroom house with a water view? At this point, you might have a knee-jerk reaction. You might prematurely decide you can't do this or have this. But exercising your capacity to decide means not rushing to this (or any) conclusion. A good decision stems only from being honest about what you want. Only then can you train your brain to see infinite possibilities rather than limitations and locked doors.

So, instead of writing off that lake-view house as too luxurious or a pipe dream, start by what I call practicing possibilities. Instead of falling back on your first, instinctive response, practicing possibilities is an exercise in looking at every option out there and really thinking each one through. Challenge yourself to brainstorm ten to twenty ways that you *could* make it happen. Go on, grab your journal. Your list could look something like this:

- Buy a lake house at X Lake.

- Rent a lake house a few months out of the year.

- Buy a duplex on the water; rent out one side and live on the other side.

- Buy a bigger house that has lake views, but at a more reasonable price.

- Buy a house that's actually on the lake but is more expensive per square foot.

- Relocate and buy a lake house in a less expensive area.

Once you've brainstormed options for what having a lake house could look like, you can also brainstorm options about how to get there financially:

- Negotiate for a raise or bonus at work.

- Start a side business.

- Get a new job with a higher salary.

- Sell your car and put that toward the down payment.

- Buy the house and then rent out the living room with the picture windows as an event space once a month to cover some of the mortgage payments.

- Wait for a year or two (or five) and keep saving.

You get the idea. Then, after you've brainstormed, ask yourself which path feels the most appealing. Visualize living out the steps involved, what you'd gain, what you'd give in exchange. Imagine all the pros and cons before making a decision. Try not to write off anything out of hand, and instead, really *see* what that option would look like if you went through with it.

Through this process, if you're fully engaging with each possibility, you'll get clarity on what specifics matter to you. Maybe you thought you had to be right on the water, but now you realize that buying the shoreline house on your ideal timeline would mean selling your car or taking on a roommate. Those trade-offs aren't worth it, so it's clear that you should instead pursue the less expensive house.

Or you may realize that you don't want what you thought you wanted at all. None of the possibilities you brainstormed feels right. You now appreciate that moving would mean putting your child into a different school district, or that you'd be far away from friends and family, or have a longer commute to work, and so on. Maybe what you want is a larger home in your current neighborhood, with more space and more privacy, and a lake vacation this summer.

Joseph and I went through this kind of decision-making process when we bought our house. We found a house we liked in a location that suited us, but we were about $15,000 short of what we'd need for the down payment. We could wait a year and save up for the down payment, or we could pull the money from another source available to us, a 401(k) loan. We just had to decide whether taking that loan would be worth it.

Now, the decision of whether or not something is worth it is never going to be just a financial decision. It's going to be a mix of costs and benefits of the impact it has on your life. So when we weighed this option, we thought holistically.

One thing that was incredibly important to us was settling down as a family. At the time, our daughter, Alexis, was going into the eighth grade. We didn't want her to have to move schools multiple times between her final year of middle school and high school. Waiting and saving wouldn't get us what we wanted there.

We also recognized that we were ahead of our savings goals. And since we were well on track to hit our long-term wealth goals, we could crunch the numbers and see that $15,000 wouldn't have much of an impact on those goals. Because the money was a loan, too, we knew we would also put that $15,000 back over time. So it's not like it would be completely lost.

Finally, we considered the fact that we weren't taking the $15,000 out and spending it. We were taking the $15,000 and leveraging it to hundreds of thousands of dollars in real estate. And while I don't generally think of our primary residence as an investment, it is still an asset that appreciates over time. The 401(k) loan would go toward securing some amount of equity in a property that we could sell later and theoretically recoup some of that money.

In the end, we decided it was worth it. Scrutinizing the trade-offs in particular helped us feel secure in that choice. Every decision we make is a give-and-take, and practicing possibilities is a great way to explore, in depth, *what* you're trading off for *what else*. When you know the answer, and you're certain about what matters to you now and in the future, you're equipped to decide.

Say you're looking to purchase a house of your own. You might weigh saving for the down payment against wanting to start a family and realize that having kids would push back your timeline to save for a 20% down payment. But you don't stop there. You ask what it would look like to have kids now *and* buy a house soon. You think through alternatives. Maybe you can go in with a lower offer, because it's not a competitive property. Maybe you can negotiate for the seller to cover some of the closing costs. Maybe you don't need to put down 20%, because your budget has room for a larger monthly mortgage payment. Whatever the case may be, you can lay out all your options, thanks to the first money capacity—understanding. Then you can decide by being open to possibility and knowing your own values. When you make a clear financial decision, what you're saying is that you understand what you're getting into, you understand the cost and the rewards, and you feel content with them. All things considered, this decision will move you in the direction you want.

It's also critical to know that part of this capacity is getting clear on how much time you want to spend making a determination. It can be tempting to hyper-optimize every financial decision you make. But all the researching, applying, and price comparing takes time—which, as we've discussed, is not something you can get back. If you enjoy getting into the nitty-gritty, then go for it. Just know that you don't have to spend more time on any given choice than you want to. You don't have to be exhaustive to exercise your capacity to decide. In fact, more time spent deliberating doesn't necessarily mean a better outcome. Even a snap judgment—listening to your instinct rather than overthinking—can be a smart use of this capacity. When you can size up the facts at hand quickly, you're using your understanding, after all. This isn't to say that you should skip practicing possibilities. It's just that you should weigh the value of your time *making* the decision as part of the process. You don't have to justify what you do to anyone but yourself.

Action Step

Identify something you want in your life, and go through the steps of practicing possibilities.

Chapter 17

EARNING

The third money capacity is *earning*. You need the capacity to make money. At the end of the day, life costs money. You want to grow your capacity to make money because making money is how you survive. And of course the goal here isn't just to survive but also to thrive. It's how you have money to shape your future into what you're dreaming of. It's how you have money to invest so that eventually you can stop working. Making money allows you to spend in all the ways that bring you joy, including being generous with others, creating a legacy, and changing the world for the better. This capacity departs from the traditional "common sense" approach to wealth building, which focuses on minimizing spending. Taken to the extreme, the "save as much as possible" approach can elevate frugal living as the only way to wealth. And again, if you're all about the minimalism and frugality, more power to you. But it's not the lifestyle for everyone. It's not the only way to build wealth, either. In fact, it's limited in how much it can accomplish.

For one thing, you can save, at maximum, only 100% of your current income—and that assumes you have literally no expenses, no grocery runs, no gas bill, no transactions within our capitalist system. Earning more, however, has unlimited potential. It's a mathematical impossibility to save more than you earn. But it's completely possible to earn 200% more, or 300% more, or 1,000% more, over time.

Finally, a savings-based strategy can compromise the second money capacity, deciding, because it's vague. It doesn't touch on specifics. It's a moving target. A true decision would go beyond saving "as much as possible" and come up with an amount, a timeline, and a goal. Frugal living can end up as a similar kind of nondecision. When practiced to the extreme, that lifestyle can push you to the point where the only option is to avoid buying, consuming, or owning. And if you have only one "right" choice, it isn't a choice at all. A short-term decision to save money might have a long-term outcome you don't really want.

Earning more keeps your options open. It allows you to practice possibilities and put your values first. When your capacity to earn expands, so do the choices in your life, both short- and long-term. If you forget your lunch at home one day, you don't have to go hungry in the name of saving. You can buy a sandwich because earning more has given you a cushion in your budget. If you want to spend your retirement traveling, you don't have to choose your destinations based on which is cheapest. You can go to the places that will bring you the most joy, because earning more expanded your travel budget. Of course, you can still live a minimalist, no-frills lifestyle if you want to. Maybe you have no desire to own a home and you love the freedom of renting, but you want to be able to buy ethically and sustainably sourced products that tend to cost more because those companies compensate their workers fairly at every level. You can strengthen your capacity to earn no matter how you choose to live. The point is that you get to *choose*. If minimalism stops feeling right for you, you have the power to try new things, upgrade parts of your life, or shift your priorities around to reflect your deepest values.

Some people don't exercise this capacity at all because they assume their ability to earn is fixed. They default to increasing their saving because that feels like something they can control. In reality, your potential to earn more is unlimited. Remember, everything in your career is a choice, from your degree to your industry to where and for whom you're working. You made those choices before, and you now make different ones in the service of this capacity. The core is once again about your openness to possibility. Earning more can start as simply as asking "What would it look like if . . . ?"

You don't have to make major departures from your current setup to increase your income, either. The most obvious place to start is asking for a raise. Revisit your job description and note where you've been excelling. Find the ways your individual work has directly contributed to the company's success. Maybe you increased profits, or decreased slowdowns. Research what similar companies are paying new hires in comparable roles. Then set up a conversation with your boss. Mention your job performance and show how you have helped the company succeed. In one conversation, you could walk away with several thousand dollars more per year—or, at the very least, it will be top of mind for your boss when the time is right.

If you can't ask for a raise, you can still grow this capacity by laying the groundwork for a higher salary down the road. Talk with your boss about how you can contribute more to a specific goal, or how to improve your trajectory in general. Ask to regroup in three to six months to discuss your progress, and track your efforts and results until then. When you have your meeting, you can point to specific benefits you brought your employer and make a case for a raise. Even if it's a no, you'll have grown your capacity to earn because you now have a record of exactly what you bring to the table that could help you get a higher-paying position elsewhere.

If you can't earn more in your current position, you can exercise your earning capacity by choosing to find a new job. Switching employers can get you a 10% to 15% raise without altering too much else about your life. You could be doing the exact same thing that you're doing now, but for more money. Joseph and I have both used this strategy over the years, and we more than doubled our income in the seven or so years after law school. Now, to get those raises, we had to move to three different states and work for five different companies, which was a lot of change, but we thought through each switch before deciding, and for us they were worth it. We always aimed to trade up to a new employer that not only paid well but also offered internal advancement opportunities so that our choice would build momentum over time. Keeping your résumé fresh, actively networking, and looking ahead are as important to your capacity to earn as salary negotiations are.

You can also grow this capacity by learning new skills or switching fields. Anything from pursuing a new degree to completing an online certification can position you to earn more. Consider switching jobs or industries, or looking for internal opportunities at your current employer. You can even leverage your current job to gain skills: Ask your supervisor about cross-training and collaboration with another department, or see if there's an employee education stipend.

It's smart to expand your capacity to earn outside of your employment, too. Maybe you have a productive hobby that could bring in another stream of income (like crafting or other DIY activities). Maybe you have a skill to offer (like portrait photography, tutoring, or refereeing a sports league). If your main job has flexible and/or part-time hours, maybe you pick up a gig on the weekends. Or you could go all in and start a business. Create products and solutions, package them, and charge for them until you earn the salary you want. You can launch an online business with little or no capital, so the risks are low. Remember, you have special gifts and expertise that can provide real value to others.

Your capacity to earn is under your control and it is all but limitless. These are only a few of the many ways you can choose to generate more money. It's time again to practice possibilities and figure out which options make sense for you and your goals. No matter where you are now, your capacity to earn is not restricted by anything other than your own desire to explore.

Action Step

Reflect on the following questions:

- How do I currently make money?

- How can I push for higher pay in my current profession?

- How can I maximize my earning potential?

- How can I hone my skills and make sure I am always in demand in my industry?

- How can I continue to make money even if I lose my job or lose another major source of income? What are some ways I can make money without being employed?

- What special talents do I have, regardless of whether I choose to monetize them? In what ways have I already used those talents to shape my life and my community into something closer to my values?

Chapter 18

HAVING

The fourth money capacity is *having*. You need to get comfortable with having money. Letting it sit there. Not immediately spending it. Just . . . having. Having money means giving yourself the time to exercise other capacities, like understanding and deciding. It means you feel at peace with wherever you are and not in a rush to act for action's sake. It means you see a situation clearly and in context. When you master having money, holding money, and not touching money, you're on track for long-term financial progress.

Lots of people are surprised at how hard it is to simply have money. They're used to feeling a rush, and resisting that rush can feel strange and uncomfortable. This is especially true if you have lived paycheck to paycheck for much of your life. Your decision-making process might look like "Will spending this overdraw my account?" If yes, then you do your best not to spend, drawing hard on your willpower. If no, then there's a sense of relief. Your willpower can relax. You won't get slapped with a fee. So you want to spend that money now, before another bill pops up and "claims" it.

I'm familiar with the urge to rush. For about a decade, I would "save" $50 at the end of the pay period, only to end up transferring it right back into my checking account when the next bill came in. In the years since, I've worked on my capacity for having money. Now, I still feel that urge when I see deposits into our business bank account, but I'm able to pause and ask myself what the big rush is. The answer, of course, is there is no rush. No matter where you are in your journey, having makes a difference.

Having money isn't exactly the same as saving. When I was "saving" $50, it was quick and easy. I just initiated a transfer from my checking account to my savings account. It took maybe five minutes. At the end, I got a check mark or a "Transaction Complete" notification. The bank told me when I was done. The money was saved. Having money isn't something you can complete in the same way. There's no check mark or notification to let you know when you're "done." Having means you can feel comfortable holding on to that money as long as it makes sense for you. It means you're comfortable defining "as long as it makes sense" for yourself.

Having also isn't the same as not spending. It means spending the money that it makes sense to spend, when it makes sense to spend it. Conversely, it means *not* spending money that *doesn't* make sense for a particular expense. It means having money set aside for different purposes, and not borrowing from one to cover another.

Here's an example I've seen with some of our members in Wealth Builders Society. They've done a nice job building up an emergency fund (which you'll learn about in part 5). They know not to raid it every month. Their capacity to have is growing. The challenge comes when a big expense arises. Maybe they bring in their car for annual inspection, and it needs new brake pads and tires, so they quite reasonably withdraw from their emergency fund to cover it.

But let's say they'd expanded their capacity to have beyond that emergency fund. They know their car is getting geriatric. They know that the inspection happens once a year. They even know exactly when that inspection is due. So they know they need to have money ready to cover that eventual cost separate from their emergency fund. An emergency is something out of the blue like a job loss, a serious illness, a housing loss, a pandemic. A routine car repair is foreseeable. Having money means setting aside enough for both expenditures. The same way you can grow your capacity to let your savings account sit instead of raiding it each month, you can grow your capacity to have money earmarked for specific, distinct expenses. That's a major way that having sets you up for long-term success and wealth.

A while back, someone posted in our Facebook group about saving her first month's emergency fund. I asked her how she and her husband planned to celebrate, and she said she hadn't thought about it. They were so focused on the next goal that they didn't even pause to feel good about *this* one. This is easy to do. It's human nature to focus on the gap between where we are and where we want to be. That feeds motivation. But motivation shouldn't come at the expense of appreciation for the now. Having money means you can feel that appreciation rather than immediately jumping into your next action. You deserve to sit with your success.

Start growing your capacity to have money right now. Take the time to be present and enjoy all the things your money is affording you right now. Reflect on the life that your money has allowed you to craft for yourself. Feel good right where you, and your money, are.

Action Steps

Get a $100 bill and carry it around in your wallet. Do not spend it. Practice having it.

Create an automatic transfer that puts a certain amount into savings every month, even if it's only $5. Do not touch this money. The amount doesn't matter—what matters is that you practice having.

Chapter 19

SPENDING

Our fifth money capacity is *spending*. Yes, you need to be able to spend money. You need to be comfortable spending on the things that bring you joy. Spending effectively doesn't mean spending or not spending a certain amount, or spending on a set of specific things. It means spending with intention, not on autopilot. It means spending in alignment with what you want, not what someone else wants or thinks. This capacity is what builds the life you want now and puts you on the path to the life you want later. It's a capacity that keeps you grounded.

Spending is another capacity that people tend to find surprisingly difficult. They get caught up in the assumption that being "good" with money means never spending it. Developing spending capacity is about resisting that black-and-white thinking. You give yourself permission to spend on the things that matter to you and bring you joy.

Your capacity to spend has nothing to do with the amount of money you pay for this or that, or how often. It has everything to do with being intentional. A price is relative. Knowing what it costs doesn't tell you how much *you* will value and savor it. If I asked if you'd enjoy a $3,000 vacation, you'd probably say something like "That depends. Where's the vacation?" If you love snorkeling and hate the cold, a $3,000 trip to the Cayman Islands would make you a lot happier than a $3,000 trip to Norwegian ski country. Spending effectively means judging on more than just price. It means you don't default to the cheapest option, or to the most expensive. It means you think about what you want out of the expense, and spend to make that happen.

On the flip side, growing this capacity means *not* spending on autopilot. Autopilot or habitual spending isn't intentional spending, and intention starts with awareness. Look at your habits and ask if they're in alignment with what you want. Did you spend that money with your goals in mind? Or did the spending just sort of . . . happen? For example, lots of our members in Wealth Builders Society realize they're autopilot spending on eating out. Eating out is a wonderful place to spend with intention, but an easy place to end up spending by default. Spending with intention would look like thinking about when, where, how often, and how much you want to eat out every month. Maybe you plan a rotation of your favorite restaurants, or maybe you have a standing weekly date at your neighborhood spot. Spending by default means not pausing to make a choice or consider options. When you stop to think about it, maybe you realize that your takeout didn't bring you any more joy than something you'd make at home, even factoring in the time you saved. If you could do it over again with intention, you would have chosen differently. (Or maybe after reviewing how often you take out dinner, you say, "Yep, totally worth the expense to avoid doing dishes twice this week," and move on to assessing your other habits.)

Reflecting on your habits helps you skip those "wouldn't do that again" moments the next time one comes along. Strengthening your capacity to spend means identifying where your spending isn't aligned with your intention, and realigning it. Maybe you don't want to eat out ten times a month—maybe five times a month is enough to get all the joy you want out of the experience, and the rest of that spending can go into your vacation fund, or your charity fund, or your massage fund, or whatever is most important to you.

As you shift money away from spending out of habit, you do want to be sure to have a plan for what you *will* spend it on. A plan gives you specific steps to spend with intention so that you don't fall back on your default settings because you're not sure what to do next. (We'll get into the specifics of spending plans in chapter 30.) For now, practice giving yourself permission to spend on things that matter to you. Nobody else has to live your life but you. Nobody else has to live with your budget. You get to choose what you value.

Start this process by getting clear on what you want. Start general, then get more granular. For instance, instead of having a vague sense that it'd be nice to have someone *else* do the cooking for your family, break that down. What you want is a personal chef who will prepare lunch and dinner for your family five days a week and deliver the meals to your home. Five lunches and five dinners for four family members means forty weekly meals in total.

Once you have your criteria, find out how much this would cost: google, send emails, talk to service providers, get quotes. Then pause. Give yourself space so you don't automatically choose the cheapest option (or the most expensive one) out of reflex. Use your capacity to decide to think through the choices in front of you. Then, reconnect with the value and joy you'll get out of this expenditure. Maybe you examine those quotes and think it sounds reasonable, and you sign yourself up. Or maybe you wonder if you really do want to redirect *that* much from your vacation goal, and conclude that one or two meals a week would be fine. Or you might feel a bit of sticker shock, which is a normal part of building your spending capacity. When you notice thoughts popping up like "That's overindulgent" or "People pay *how much*?!" pause again. Consider where those thoughts are coming from. Do *you* feel that way? Deep down, do you agree with your knee-jerk reaction? That's all that matters. You earned your money, you get to spend it, and you are the one getting something in return.

A strong spending capacity means you aren't spending based on other people's opinions. Someone else might not want to have a personal chef. That's a question for them, their values, and their money. You're going to look at *your* values. Maybe you value taking care of yourself with healthy food. Maybe you value a real sit-down family dinnertime instead of feeling rushed and stressed out to get dinner on the table. Maybe you value supporting small local businesses. Maybe you value the free time you get by not having to meal plan. Spend money to live those values. As long as you plan for the expense, then you don't have to think about anything else.

Spending isn't just about living values in the present, either. The way you spend now can help future you live those values, too. Investing in a personal trainer might save you thousands on medical bills later. Upgrading to a business-class ticket can bring you home from vacation feeling rested instead of frazzled. Shopping for holiday gifts at nearby boutiques instead of online can help keep your local business district thriving and vibrant. Quite often, when you pay more (for a high-quality product or service), you're doing something better not just for yourself, but for the community and the planet, too. Spend with intention for both the immediate and the long term.

The capacity to spend keeps you grounded, grateful, and present. Remember, life is the thing that happens between your goals. Even as you're working to achieve financial freedom, or to buy a house, or to put your kids through college, you're still going through life one moment at a time. The day-to-day moments are what make memories.

They're what you will look back on with joy, not the day when your retirement account hit a certain number. Spend to bring yourself those moments of joy.

Action Step

Buy something you want and practice savoring that purchase. Slow down and feel it. What did you buy? How does it make you feel? How are you relishing everything that's great about it? What personal values does it connect you to?

Chapter 20

LOSING

We all try so hard to not *lose* money. But it's impossible to go through life without losing money somewhere along the way. You're going to buy an appliance that breaks and needs replacing. You're going to take a job in a different city, spend time and money moving, only to get downsized and have to do it all in reverse. Or you're *not* going to take that job in a new city because of your relationship, but when that relationship ends, you're mad because you left money on the table for nothing.

Even if you make thoughtful and solid choices, you're still subject to the whims of the universe. You're going to move when the rent in your neighborhood quadruples. You're going to lose a chunk of your net worth when the market falls. You're going to be stuck in stasis because of a global pandemic. You might not know the specifics of what's going to happen, but you can be sure that something *will* happen to cause you a loss.

Losing money is a fact of life. Still, when it happens, it feels like a catastrophe. Your emotions kick in, and that causes you to make choices out of fear, out of lack, out of scarcity. When you're in a state of panic, your advanced brain goes off-line, your instinctive brain takes over, and you're not able to access the highest levels of decision-making.

Getting comfortable losing money doesn't mean you will take constant risks, of course. You should still be choosy about when you roll the dice. You don't have to risk everything—but you need to be willing to risk something. Every decision comes with unknowns. Investing in an advanced degree so that you can uplevel your career and earn more in the long run is a calculated risk. Starting a side hustle? That's a risk. Purchasing a condo that you intend to rent out to tenants? That's a risk. Taking on more challenges at work so you can push for a raise in six months? That's a risk. All of these have likely upsides, but also a chance of downsides. We take calculated risks every day by just getting out of bed in the morning; it's a natural part of life.

Wrap your mind around the notion that you can lose money and still be successful, which will allow you to take the risks that are part of building wealth. You always pivot as the world pivots around you because you know you're capable of adapting.

Otherwise, if you're too afraid of losing money, you're more likely to make decisions that feel safe but aren't in your best interest. You live smaller than you want to because you're so afraid. For example, fear of losing money stops a lot of people from investing. They worry that the markets are going to tank and they're going to lose a chunk of their net worth.

Well, that might happen. That *has* happened, in fact.

When the market dropped at the start of the pandemic, our portfolio decreased by about 40% in one day. It was the most significant single-day loss we'd *ever* experienced. But although it was shocking to see how much the market dropped, it also provided an opportunity for us to teach and coach this capacity. Joseph and I were able to help normalize and explain to our Wealth Builders Society members how to think about these types of inevitable short-term fluctuations, as well as walk them through the types of plans that they, and anyone, can put in place to help mitigate the risk. We were also able to help them work through their emotions, which is a key part of this capacity. When these upheavals happen, it's normal to experience emotional swings, too, but staying grounded in your personal financial reality and understanding can keep you centered. You don't have to let public sentiment have an undue influence on how you feel about your own finances.

This incident also shows how the capacity to understand will build your capacity to lose. When the market dropped, I knew what was happening. I knew, for one, that the hiccup was just that, a hiccup. It was temporary, like all the ups and downs of the market. I knew I was still decades away from retirement and had time to ride it out. I knew I wasn't going to sell shares in my portfolio anytime soon, so the present value wasn't a pressing concern. I knew I still owned the same number of shares even if their value had shifted.

Even if you're already investing, the fear of losing money can make you catastrophize and imagine your losses to be more devastating than they are. If you are comfortable with losing, you can stay clearheaded and look at the facts instead.

So when our portfolio dropped, I crunched the numbers. I wanted to see what I'd need to do in case the market didn't recover quickly—how much would I need to increase our savings to put us back on track? The answer: We'd have to save an extra $150 a month for five years. That felt doable.

Mastering this capacity means recognizing that these things will happen. But it also means recognizing that a loss doesn't mean that you are bad with money, or that you're never going to be able to make more money, or that you won't reach your goals. All it means is that the unpredictable happened, or you tried something and it didn't work. Either way, you have new information that you can assimilate and use to make choices going forward.

We grow by trying and failing. You can still reach your goals, even with those losses, and you'll make it so much easier on yourself if you can resist beating yourself up in resentment, regret, frustration, or anger. None of those emotions help: What's done is done. When you're good at losing money, you don't let your emotional math get ahead of the actual math.

Being at peace with potential loss is a capacity that pays off every day. If you are unwilling to try a new restaurant or new cuisine because maybe you'll hate the food, then you will never get to experience the joy of warm, buttery roti bread or a refreshing Caribbean sorrel drink. If you are unwilling to apply for a promotion because you don't want to risk rejection, then there's one thing I can guarantee—you won't get that promotion. Sure, you protected your ego from discomfort, but you waved goodbye to a $30,000 salary increase.

When you are extremely risk-averse, you may think you are protecting yourself and your funds, but you're doing the opposite. You are inviting in less abundance and less security, not more. Don't let fear of loss drive your decisions, because undifferentiated fear doesn't lead us to our best outcomes. Instead, use that fear to keep yourself safe and avoid *unnecessary* risks, in tandem with your capacities to understand and decide.

When you expand your capacity to tolerate risk and loss, you avoid getting locked into stagnancy. You welcome potential and possibility.

Action Step

Consider some of these questions:

- When I lose money, what am I making that loss mean? What emotions come up?

- When I lose money, or consider losing money, what am I afraid of? (E.g., "I will never get this money back," "I will never recover financially.")

- How can I find gratitude for a past loss? What have I gained or learned from it?

Chapter 21

GROWING

The final money capacity is *growing*. It's not enough to earn money; you also need to invest it and let it work for you. This capacity means you know where you're starting from and where you want to end up, and you feel good about both. You understand what investing really means, what it looks like in practice, and why it works. And you take action to create a solid wealth-building plan that grows your money on autopilot.

Your capacity to grow starts by making peace with starting where you are. You've already learned about the time value of money, and using this capacity means making that principle work for you. As a brief refresher, the time value of money means that the longer you wait to invest, the more you'll have to invest to reach the same target. When you use this capacity, you embody the proverb, "The best time to plant a tree is twenty years ago. The next best time is today."

To grow your money most effectively, you also have to know where you're going. That means adopting a long-term mindset, because growing is all about the future. You already know that it is critical to build a nest egg to support yourself and your desired lifestyle in retirement. This capacity is what will get you there, and investing is the best way to build that nest egg. Investing is how you become an "inevitable millionaire." Yes, millionaire. Even a multimillionaire. Maybe the idea of becoming a millionaire feels new and strange to you because it's hard to see exactly how to get from where you are now to having multiple-comma bank balances. Well, here's an analogy that might help. The average American eats approximately one ton of food a year. If you think about sitting down to eat a ton of food, of course there's no way it's going to fit in your stomach all at once. But bit by bit, by eating three square meals every day for 365 days in a row, you can get there without even thinking about it. Becoming a millionaire works in the exact same way. By investing small amounts consistently over time, it's simple and doable. That multimillion-dollar investment account isn't a giant food mountain you have to tackle all at once. It's something you build up through small, consistent action over time.

Mindset and goals are one part of this capacity, but practical knowledge of what investing looks like is key as well. To be clear, investing does not mean gambling in the stock market. Maybe you saw the headlines about GameStop stock or the cryptocurrency explosion and concluded that investing is always boom or bust. But the investment vehicles that make headlines are outliers by definition. That's what makes them interesting stories. A real capacity to grow means seeing the full landscape of investing beyond the sensationalist reports. You don't need to be a stock market genius or adrenaline junkie. You don't need to comb financial news every hour, or day-trade options, or go deep into stock-tips online forums. You don't have to take any giant risks at all. All there really is to "being an investor" is putting a solid wealth-building plan in place that takes advantage of time.

Your capacity to grow money requires you to take action. The key is to be proactive and not reactive. You simply need to get in the habit of investing regularly, even automatically. Find ways to make a regular contribution as frictionless as possible. If that means an automatic withdrawal of $20 per month to start, then set it up. It's better to start with a smaller amount than not to start at all, or even to delay starting. The habit alone is just as valuable as the returns you'll get. Not being reactive, on the other hand, means sticking to your plan even during market uncertainty. Think of this as a specialized application of your capacity to lose. You can start practicing this right away, too. Get in the practice of keeping a cool head and not making investing decisions from an emotional place when your portfolio is still small, and the skill will grow as your money does. The sooner you start these habits and mindset shifts, the faster you'll expand this capacity.

A strong capacity to grow also means taking the long view. That means prioritizing wealth building even though retirement isn't as immediate as other expenses. Pay yourself first, even before paying off debt. As I've mentioned before, you don't have to be debt-free to build wealth. You can do both at the same time. Beyond that, you'll be able to address your debt, whatever it is, over the years. Funding your retirement is distinct. Once you're approaching that age, you won't have that power of time available in the same way. It's tempting to focus on paying off debt because it's more emotionally immediate. You already have (or have experienced) whatever that debt got you. The number feels attached to something concrete, like a house, an education, a car, months of credit card purchases. You know how you feel about those things already. Meanwhile, you don't yet know how you'll feel enjoying your retirement. You can only imagine it. But your capacity to grow means that, once again, you're not letting that emotional math get in the way of the financial math. You are doing what it takes to make your money work for you.

Growing your money means knowing that you're not compromising your big, long-term goals to serve short-term ones. At the end of the day, you are the one who has to live with your financial decisions, so no one else's "rules" apply here. I want you to have the capacity to grow your money, however you invest, because I want you to have an abundant life. I want you to enjoy your days now *and* build that multiple seven-figure nest egg to support you later on, whatever abundance looks like for you.

Action Step

Set aside thirty minutes in your calendar at some point over the next week to start researching different investment options and becoming familiar with them. Google whatever questions you have or terms you want to know more about.

PART 4

DEFINE YOUR RICH LIFE

Chapter 22

YOU ONLY GET ONE LIFE

H appy endings are wished for and earned, not granted at random. Even for Disney princesses.

Think about it: At the beginning of every Disney movie, the future princess is trying to get something, do something, or make something happen, right? She belts a big "I want" song about her heart's desire. She's *not* content with the status quo, whether it's being locked in a tower or staying on her home island or living a provincial life. She has a dream, and she keeps reaching for that dream against all the odds.

That's how Disney princesses get their happily-ever-after, prince or no prince, fairy godmother notwithstanding. They work for it. They resist the paths set before them and fight for what they want. Yes, these are just movies, but they teach us a real lesson about the power of knowing your dream and stepping off the preordained path.

In the real world, we're (mostly) not singing to bluebirds or battling a magical curse, but we do tend to have a series of milestones we're trying to hit on the supposed road to happiness. Too many of us follow that path without listening to our inner voice. We don't take a moment to know ourselves or our dreams. We don't have any "I want" songs to sing. It's not until we're pretty far down that path that we may realize we don't even *like* it. Hello, midlife crisis.

The default path is not the only one available to you. The path to the best version of your life is out there—but only you can chart it. No one else can or will do it for you. If you want to raise the odds of living out your dreams, then you have to design your life on purpose. And only then will your money truly serve you in creating joy and abundance.

This doesn't necessarily mean doing more, working more, or constantly striving for more and more and more. It just means being in tune with what a good life looks like for you. Instead of wandering through your days with no clear sense of your values, or living for other people's values instead of your own, you can walk in alignment with who you want to be in that moment and who you want to become in the future.

If you're struggling even to picture a big dream right now, that's okay, and that's normal. Most of us aren't trained to see the whole realm of possibility. The specific steps on our predetermined paths might look different, depending on what we've been taught to see as "success." But whether the steps are high school, college, career, or settling down, getting married, and having kids, there's always *something* laid out. There's no step for pausing and considering if we're even moving in the right direction. There's no option to try out a different direction, or loop back and take a left turn, because those are seen as failures. There isn't often space for self-reflection at all.

It's time to make that space for yourself. You can get more comfortable with trial and error, and learn what lights you up through experience. You can get attuned to that inner voice and discover what matters to you deep down. Because if you're not living with intention, you're living by default. Many people believe that they'll be happy only when they've hit certain financial milestones, that if they work hard enough and save up enough, there will come a time when they'll simply stop worrying about money. Only *then* can they think about things like dreams and goals. As a result, they end up with hollow victories; they're making progress on their finances, but something still feels off. They don't feel as satisfied as they thought they would.

If you've found yourself in that situation, it's not because you're acting against your best interests. You're not self-sabotaging or actively squashing your dreams. You're probably just doing what you think is right. Somewhere, you picked up the idea that the way to be a real adult/a good parent/a responsible citizen is to be practical, to *not* chase your dreams. And you further picked up the idea that the way to be practical is to follow money rules—because. If you have a partner or children, you might even feel obligated to put "family first" and give everything you can to the family unit (and this is true for men and women alike).

I want you to know that whatever road you've been walking or see before you isn't the only one. I want you to know that it's okay to have dreams that are big and ambitious and exciting and all your own. I want you to start recognizing that inner voice, the one that tells you what's working and what's not working. I want you to shape your everyday life and your long-term goals on purpose, not by default.

Because you only get one life.

When you think about that one life you have, that one life that's all yours, you can start to see how staying on the default path doesn't make sense. The default path expects you to spend all your energy and time on reaching those predefined steps. It tells you that when those boxes are checked, *then* you can make your own plans. *Then* you can start dreaming of where you truly want to go. But it's your time and your energy, neither of which you can get back once you've spent it. It should go toward building what *you* want it to, every step of the way.

Your time and energy should always move you closer to where you want to go. The default path, by definition, is never personally tailored. But it's not enough just to jump off that default path, either. You still have to define where you want to end up. After all, if you don't know where you're going, you'll never know when or if you arrive. No one gets in their car and says, "Well, I don't know what I need, or where to get it, but let's see what happens if I fire up the engine and start driving." You need a destination before you pull out of the driveway, whether it's a quick errand to the store or a cross-country road trip. Otherwise, it's just a waste of gas.

Again: You only get *one* life. Your time is limited, just like everyone else's. Money helps you make the most of your time, but it can't make you *more* time. There are limitations at every level of financial success, and even the richest person in the world cannot have everything.

Because you only get one life.

No one ever gets to stop thinking about money, or making trade-offs, or prioritizing. But when you can make those trade-offs, when you're comfortable with what you want and what you value, that's when abundance sets in. When you're clear on your values and goals, you'll be able to tell if any given choice is getting you closer to that finish line, and maybe you'll choose differently.

Making trade-offs isn't always easy or comfortable, and that discomfort is why many people don't set their own value system when it comes to financial decision-making. Perhaps they suspect that honestly answering the question "What do I *really* want?" will open a can of worms. Knowing what they want might mean they'll feel compelled to go after it. They might have to make changes—maybe a lot of changes. They might have a certain level of financial security and not want to rock the boat. Or they might have a modest income and not feel equal to the task of earning more to support their ideal lifestyle. They might just have to face the fact that *everything* is a choice—their job, their house, their children, their partner or spouse—and they aren't maintaining that status quo because they have to but because they *choose* to.

With all that on the line, it can feel safer to tell yourself you have no agency. That the future is when you'll finally be able to enjoy life, not right now. But it *is* possible. It's also essential, and it's empowering.

Every stage of life has its unique moments of beauty. But if you're focused only on getting to some imagined future, you can miss them rather than being present while they're happening. When I was a new mom, I was always thinking about what was next. I was planning and taking action for *later*. I didn't have everything I wanted yet. But I was able to remind myself to enjoy the little moments. I loved being with Alexis, pushing her on the swings, snuggling her little baby face, drawing pictures together in her nursery, entertaining her. All that was happiness. I was living a life I loved.

That was possible because of my circumstances, not in spite of them. I was out of the cockroach-infested apartment, but money was still tight. No expensive toys or outings meant spending more time with Alexis one-on-one. I knew she wasn't going to be a baby forever, and my human experience wouldn't be complete if I didn't make the most of the time we had together, just the two of us. It was an empowering time, too, because I knew that, in each moment, I was choosing what I wanted. I was both finding joy in my day-to-day and laying the groundwork for the years to come. That's what I mean when I say that we only get one life: Seek balance. Enjoy the now *and* look forward to the future.

It's a natural tendency to look at a future destination that we need to reach in order to be happy. Many of us don't even think about the present except to compare it to an imagined future. We don't want to deal with here. We wish they were already there.

What we're wishing for is an impossibility. You can't get to "there" any way except through all the years in between. But the bigger wish, the wish for a life of abundance and joy, *is* possible. Life isn't a fairy tale, but there is magic to be found in every part of your journey. It's just up to you to discover it. Every day is an opportunity to be intentional with how you're living right now. Because you get to enjoy every moment of your life, not just the moments when you've accomplished a goal.

Learn to live richly—right now. Remember to enjoy your whole life, every year and every season, because no one knows how many years we're going to get. Most of all, know that you can create a life that looks and feels exactly the way you want it to, no matter how much is in your checking account right now.

You have the power to do that. It's going to take time, but you *can* start in this very instant. Consider which trade-offs you can make immediately to completely transform your life—not tomorrow, today. It is possible to enjoy your life at every stage of your journey, while still working toward that idealized vision of your future.

All you have to do is start.

Chapter 23

YOUR LIFE VISION

How close is your life right now to the life that you *want* to live—your ideal life?

If you're realizing that you haven't ever stopped to think about what that would even look like, then you're not alone. Too often, people put off enjoying today, surrounded by the things and experiences they want, until some far-off future without fleshing out what that future holds. They don't look for ways to start incorporating aspects of that ideal version of their lives into their current lives, because they don't have a clear vision for it. When I've asked clients *why* they haven't stopped to delineate a vision for the future, they have to pause and think. They've never realized that it's something they *should* do.

When we're young, we're thinking about our future all the time. We're encouraged to dream big. We're asked what we want to be when we grow up. We talk with our classmates about what college we want to go to, what major we want to study, and what profession will come after. But then we grow up and all of that just . . . stops. Suddenly, we're adults with a career, steps laid out into the horizon, responsibilities and expectations to meet. With no one reminding us to continue to dream and change and reach for what we want to be when we "grow up," many of us forget that we're still growing. We're still as capable of transforming our lives in new and interesting ways. The possibilities may not be endless, but they are abundant and just as available to you as they were when you were a child. You only need to remember how to look for them.

Maybe you recognize that the possibilities are out there, but you still feel stuck. Dreaming big feels risky. It feels scary. As a kid, a big dream is exciting, but it's also a safe distance away. There are no real expectations or stakes. As an adult, a dream can feel like just another potential failure. But fear of failure is to fail in advance. Because if you don't try something, you're guaranteed not to accomplish it. When life-altering dreams bubble up in your mind, don't default to that fear. Ask yourself: "Would I rather look back on having tried and failed, or look back on all the missed opportunities I never went for?"

Or maybe you just feel busy. There's so much else that needs attention. But figuring out what you want from your "one wild and precious life" is one of the best ways you can prioritize and use your time. Maybe instead of watching an entire movie tonight, you pause Netflix at the halfway point and spend the other half of your TV time envisioning the movie of your best life. Letting your imagination dream up all the wonderful things you want can be just as entertaining as watching *Bachelor in Paradise*. Even easier, let yourself fantasize as you go about your day. What would you upgrade, given the chance? What would you swap out? Think of the exercise as something fun, because it is fun. When you let your imagination run wild, a kind of butterfly effect takes over. You'd love to get weekly pedicures at your favorite salon, but it's a twenty-minute bus ride away and that's not ideal for wet toes. What if you had a car and could drive there instead? Well, your apartment doesn't have parking. What if you moved into that new high-rise across the street?

Anything and everything is on the table. Once again, practice possibilities. If that little voice starts muttering about how it's too expensive or a waste of time, just gently hush it for now. You will get to the practicalities later.

At this point, some people still hesitate. Maybe their vision starts to form in their mind, but they don't know how they could ever get from point A to point B. And because they don't know the *how*, they don't even want to consider the *what*.

But you don't *have* to know how you'll get all the way to that vision. You just have to find the next, smallest step in its direction.

Remember that Henry Ford quote: "Whether you think you can, or think you can't, you're right." That holds here as well. When you shy away from your vision because it "seems impossible" or is "too much," you're quitting before you even start. You are turning the fact that you don't have the *how* into a self-fulfilling prophecy.

But when you set the vision for your life, you're just opening a door. When you allow your brain to want what it wants, you subconsciously fire it up to look for ways to get there. You'll start to notice opportunities you would have shut out or ignored otherwise. You'll walk by that new building and grab a flyer about available units. You'll spot a car with a FOR SALE sign and save the number to call later. You'll read about an internal promotion opportunity at work and go through the job description instead of trashing the email.

You know that there are wonderful, exciting wishes in your heart. Things you want to do. Things you want to experience. Things you want to try. Maybe a new career that you want to transition into or a new town that you'd love to live in one day. Things you've enjoyed and want to make part of your everyday routine. Maybe you've always wanted to open a tea shop or move to that cute coastal town that would be an amazing place for your kids to grow up. The more specific and detailed you can make those wishes, the better you define what's involved, and the more likely you are to take action.

I want you to have a distinct, defined sense of what your "rich life" looks like, both right now and in your future. I want you to really *see* that ideal life that looks and feels exactly the way you want it to, a life that you define for yourself. This exercise isn't about delaying gratification or waiting until you reach some far-off goal before you can be happy. It's about identifying what you want so you can show up every day in a way that helps forge it. Remember, the goal is to create a holistic plan that allows you to build a life you love right now, while also creating wealth for your future.

It's time to envision, then.

Try this: Imagine that you are one hundred years old, and you're on your deathbed. (Stick with me.) You're surrounded by the people you love, feeling relaxed, at peace, full of gratitude. You're looking back on your amazing life, which was so full and joyous that you can't imagine it any other way. You left no stone unturned. You went after all your dreams and you lived to the fullest. You can't even *think* of anything more you'd have wanted to do.

What does that life look like? What did you do? What did you experience? What did you see? Who did you love? Who were you surrounded by over the course of your life? What did you devote your career to? What were your passions, your accomplishments, your failures—and what did you learn from them? What in your full and beautiful life has your one-hundred-year-old self grinning from ear to ear at how amazing it was?

Keep in mind that while your vision for your future is what lights the way to your best life, it can, and will, also change over time. That is okay. Once upon a time, my long-term vision included becoming a Supreme Court justice, and now it is centered on building a company that allows me to do work that changes lives. I still feel good about the choices I made along the way because I know I made them with the most recent version of my vision in mind. That's why you'll want to revisit these exercises over time—at least yearly—to keep in touch with what your best future looks like.

If you're still not sure about what you want, or if you need another way of shaping this vision, don't worry. It's not always easy to pinpoint your true desires, especially if you're not used to envisioning them on a grand scale. You can shape your sense of your richest life, in all senses of the word, starting with exactly where you are in the present, too.

Get out that journal again and consider your life right now. What's going on? What's working and what's not working? Set aside envisioning the future. Just look at your life as it is, and think about what aspects you want to rework. These are the areas that are frustrating, or don't make you happy, or simply aren't exactly the way you want them to be. Finding what I call *areas of opportunity* can empower you, because you've defined exactly what could be different instead of getting stuck in a vague feeling of powerlessness.

When it comes to what *is* working in your life, this exercise helps you understand what's getting you excited right now. Knowing what brings you joy is key to knowing what to prioritize in your one-year spending plan (which we'll get to in chapter 30). But it also gives you a starting point to, for example, have conversations with your significant other about what lights you up and to make joint spending decisions accordingly.

No matter how you shape your vision of your ideal life, it's powerful to put it down in words. It can help you prioritize your next steps and gain clarity on where you're going. I did this practice a few years back when I was still working as a lawyer. I'd just found out that I was slated to be part of a team that would write the next major financial regulation in the US. But at the same time, One Big Happy Life was growing quickly, and the long commute to DC every day was draining. Did I want to go all in on my legal career? Or did I want to jump ship and become a full-time entrepreneur? I thought about what I envisioned for my life. I knew I wanted time with my family. I wanted to help people create lives that they love while also building wealth. And I knew the commute and long hours of my day job were not getting me closer to either of those ambitions. Well, you can guess which decision I made, and it was absolutely the right one.

Here's how you can apply your vision to evaluate the trade-offs whenever you see a fork in the road. First, identify the friction points involved in each option. The nature of a trade-off is that friction is inevitable, so the goal is the friction point that either doesn't bother you as much as the other choice or is worth it to get you to a certain result. If you're thinking about buying a house in the city versus the countryside, for example, the friction points on one end of the scale might be the noise and the lack of space, while the others are no more overnight Amazon Prime and a long drive to get to the nearest town. If you know you ultimately want to be in the heart of the action, in a cultural center, then the friction points of city noise and compromising on square footage are worth it. If your ideal life looks like seeing the stars at night and having your own acreage to stroll, then the friction points of longer commutes and seven-day shipping are worth it. When you get as much of what you want and as little of what you don't want, then you know the trade-off is a solid one.

Action Step

Try the one-hundred-year-old-self exercise. Set aside half an hour of dedicated time and grab a journal to write in. Spend your half hour (or more) imagining a life that your one-hundred-year-old self would reflect on with a huge smile. Use the following questions for inspiration:

- What did your life look like in your forties, fifties, and sixties? Your seventies, eighties, and nineties?

- What kinds of things did you accomplish?

- What were your fondest memories?

- Who was beside you along the way?

- What did your day-to-day life look like?

- What are you most proud of?

Journal about whatever comes to you, and be as detailed as possible. By the end, you will have a much more robust vision of your ideal life.

Chapter 24

SETTING FINANCIAL AND LIFE GOALS

Hopefully, now that you've identified your vision, you're getting excited about the life that awaits you. You might also be feeling scared and audacious for dreaming so big. Good. That means you're on the right track.

The next step is to translate that vision into tangible goals, and then to break those goals down into actionable steps. Once you've defined the actions you need to take, you can set a timeline to achieve each one, and use that timeline to measure your progress as you go. After that, all you have to do is start at the beginning.

This goal-setting process might be different from others you've tried. Many of us get very focused on the measurable aspects of our goals, and it *is* true that goals work best when they're well defined. But starting with those benchmarks doesn't do much for motivation.

For example, say you have an objective like putting $100 into a savings account every month. It's specific and has a clear time frame. But what's motivating about it? Why do you want $100 going into savings every month? What purpose is that money going to serve? Without answering these questions first, this admirable aim can easily slide into a "saving for saving's sake" habit. So, while systems and benchmarks are important, they're not what will keep you going. What will keep you motivated is that clear vision of the end result.

That's why we start with the vision for your life. Before you get specific on what you'll actually be doing, you need to know where you want those actions to take you, and why getting there matters. In his bestselling book *The 7 Habits of Highly Effective People*, businessman Stephen R. Covey coined the term *beginning with the end in mind*. This is a concept to keep top of mind as we go. Beginning with the end in mind makes it apparent right away whether any given action gets you closer to that finish line, or further from it. In that way, it gives every action you take a greater context. If you know that your monthly $100 savings is building up to fund a once-in-a-lifetime trip to Mount Kilimanjaro, you get a mini rush of anticipation for that dream vacation every time you make the transfer. The defined, intentional endgame of the trip creates a positive context around saving. Otherwise, if you're stacking up money just because, there's no meaningful context. It's a means without a real end.

Beginning with the end in mind doesn't only work for glamorous visions of your life, either. Putting context to your vision can make your everyday financial goals feel meaningful, too. Maybe you're putting that $100 into a sinking fund to absorb the costs of future appliance repairs, and you know that every dollar you save gets you closer to a life in which you don't have to panic when your fridge breaks down, because the cost of a replacement is taken care of. In that context, you feel much more motivated. You're not just throwing money into savings. You're building yourself a less-stressed future.

Starting with your life vision also makes it easier to stay flexible.

Life throws surprises at you, things happen, and you might have to adjust. When you base a goal on defined actions and benchmarks, you might have to go back to the drawing board if it is no longer feasible. Say you decide you're going to jog to the park and back three times a week. If you move to a high-rise apartment building on a busy street with no sidewalks, that's not doable anymore. But if you came up with that jogging goal based on a vision of getting into shape, you can easily pivot and sign up for a nearby gym, or get a yoga mat to use in your living room. You're still en route toward your vision because you never lost sight of it.

With that in mind, let's break that all-encompassing vision into two types of goals: financial goals and life goals. Both are essential for creating your rich life, and both cost money. Financial goals help you build stability and cover your essential needs, both now and in the future. They can include milestones like having an emergency fund and hitting your monthly minimum investing rate every month. Everyone needs to hit their financial goals, regardless of what their ideal life looks like. Everyone needs a solid financial base, and everyone will want (or need) to retire from working at some point. What varies from person to person is the amount that gets you to these milestones, such as how much you want to put in that emergency fund, or what your exact minimum investing rate is.

Life goals, on the other hand, are personal to you, and include things like where you want to live, what type of work you want to do, how many children you want to have, how much you want to travel, even what kind of car you want to drive. These are goals that bring you joy and make life special, meaningful, and fun.

Of the two categories, I've found that financial goals tend to make intuitive sense to most of us fairly quickly. Most people are already familiar with the idea of a rainy-day or emergency fund. The difference in my approach is that you want to keep your life vision top of mind even as you crunch the numbers. You want to reframe the standard "saving for saving's sake" attitude and think more in terms of building stability and minimizing risk (which we'll discuss further in chapter 26).

Life goals, on the other hand, might feel bigger, broader, or further off. The connection to your finances might not be as obvious. But remember, every decision is a financial decision. When you decide what your ideal life looks like, you're deciding on a particular financial reality. Let's say that you know you want to live in Seattle, because it has beautiful summers, a reasonable cost of living for a coastal city, and nature all around it. Just knowing where you want to live is the first step to getting more specific about what number you'll be aiming for. In this example, you know Seattle's going to be more expensive than, say, Des Moines. You also know you love waking up to the sunrise every morning, so you figure you'll want to live in a high-rise building. You can start doing research *today* on what high-rise rents are in Seattle.

This isn't just true for the major plans like where you'll live or where you'll travel or where you'll build your vacation home. Let's say you want to train for a marathon. You know you'll have to pay the entry fee for your race bib, maybe pick up some new sneakers. But that's not the only financial aspect to this goal. Making time for training could affect what types of jobs you choose to work (so that you can have time in your schedule to run) or cause you to spend more on time-savers and convenience items, like housekeeping or meal kits or extra childcare (so that your day-to-day keeps running smoothly even with this new commitment).

Both examples are based on what you want your life to look like, but they're also goals that have a financial impact, and that means you can make them measurable on two fronts: how much the goal costs, and your desired time frame for achieving it.

Let's see what that looks like in practice. Maybe you've decided "my life goal is to travel more." That doesn't fit the bill, since "more" isn't an amount, and there's no mention of a timeline. So you refine and decide you want to go on a cruise to the Bahamas by next May. That's *very* specific. With a little internet research, you can price out your dream cruise and determine it'll cost $5,000. Now you have a life goal. With a dollar amount and a deadline, you can plan, take action, and track your progress toward reaching it.

Here's another common example. Lots of people have the goal of "wanting to live comfortably." But that's too vague. For one person, that might mean an annual income of $100,000. For another, it'd be more like $1 million. Someone else might just want to literally be physically comfortable everywhere they go and have a body-size beanbag chair in every room of their house. The specifics vary, and the specifics matter. Each of these options will be quantified in different ways. Saving enough money to live on $100K a year is much easier than saving enough to live on $1 million a year. Buying a comfy chair for every room of your house is easier still.

To be clear, making your life goals measurable doesn't mean you have to be exact down to the penny. Just researching some ballpark numbers can be a quick and easy way to drill down. If you know you want to move from Arizona to Maine in a year's time, you could start by identifying the major steps you'd need to take. You'd have to find a place to live and then you'd have to move yourself and your stuff out there. Keep breaking each piece of the puzzle down until you get a rough list of line items. From there, look up the going rate for each: average housing costs in Maine, the going rate for cross-country movers, even the cost of taking a few trips to house hunt. If you have your eye on a particular vacation destination, research plane tickets, a hotel room, dining out, and so on. You can even plan how much you want to spend for your children's college education. (Granted, there's a *lot* more speculation involved there, because depending on how old your kids are, you could be looking at almost two decades into the future, but there are online calculators that you can use as a baseline so that you have some numbers to work with.) The bottom line is that even big dreams can be broken into smaller steps, everything has a price, and Google is your friend.

Another way to give your goals a dollar amount is to simply decide how much you want to spend on that particular goal. When Joseph and I decided we wanted to purchase a car for our daughter, Alexis, we first figured out how much we were willing to spend. We also thought through all the specs, like safety features, vehicle size, and so on. Then it became a matter of finding a car that fit within the budget we'd set and hit as many of those wish-list features as possible. Similarly, you might know you want to take a vacation somewhere with sunshine and white sand beaches, but you aren't attached to any one particular destination. You'd be as happy in Fiji as you would in Saint Lucia. In that case, you can decide up front how much you want to pay for your getaway, and use that number to narrow down your options.

Last, you'll want to choose the time frame in which to accomplish your goal. Often, that time frame is flexible. If you have your heart set on seeing Paris one day but haven't drilled down on the specifics, you could do that at any point in your life, even in your eighties. Other objectives are more time-bound. If you want to take your daughter to Disney World to meet Moana, you'll both probably get the most joy out of going when she's six, not *twenty*-six. College tuition is an example of a time-bound goal, too, because you'll need to make a deposit before each semester starts, and coming up short might mean canceling a vacation to free up the funds. Similarly, not having enough in the bank to make it to a family event, like a wedding, could lead you to take on unexpected credit card debt or miss the event entirely. As you nail down these timelines, try working backward from your time-bound goals and fit the more flexible ones around them.

You'll probably end up with a long list of goals, and a range of costs and timelines. And you might get the sinking feeling that your money can't stretch far enough to work on all of them at the same time. That's fine. You don't have to save for every single thing all at once. In fact, trying to work toward all thirty-five of your dreams simultaneously can be counterproductive. You'll have a lot to keep track of, which takes mental energy. Instead, prioritize.

There's no secret to deciding what to go for first, although it can feel daunting if you're not used to exercising your capacity to decide. People who aren't used to making decisions are likely unfamiliar with prioritizing, too, because they go hand in hand. This is why it's important to remember that you can't do everything at once. What you get to control is which goals get your focus and attention right now, and how your values motivate you to get there. When you can be content with the order in which *you* decide to do things, you can be at peace with prioritization.

It's also key to acknowledge that the amount you might want to spend on any given purchase or experience can shift over time. In the beginning, I only wanted to spend, say, $5,000 on a car. But now as I'm deeper into building wealth, and further along in my life and in my earning potential, I'm willing to spend more for a vehicle I really love. And you might find that holds true for you, too. So don't be afraid if how much you want to spend ticks up over time, or if some of your goals here come with price tags that might have knocked you over a few years ago. Remember, there's no inherent morality to any size, number, or price. There's only how much you value it, and how much it's worth to you.

Action Step

Grab your journal (or a big piece of paper) and sketch out three columns: one for your goals, one for the costs, and one for the time frame.

First, in the leftmost column, list your life goals, as many as you can think of. Some ideas to get you started:

- Places you want to live

- Cities or countries you want to visit

- Skills or hobbies you want to learn

- Causes or institutions you want to support

- Gifts you want to give to others

Next, look at the columns for costs and time frame. Fill out any costs or time frames you know offhand. For example, if you want to take your family to visit your parents' home country before the kids are grown, you have between now and their eighteenth birthdays, or if you want to spend at least $20,000 on a big fiftieth-anniversary party to renew your vows, then you can start there.

For the goals without obvious time frames or costs, start doing research to begin ballparking the dollar amount and thinking through the time frames in which you'd like to achieve any of them.

Once that's done, start to prioritize. Which life goals need to happen by a certain date, or at a certain time? Which financial goals are most important, and which can you build up over time?

Optional: If listing all your goals feels daunting, make it into a game with your family or your partner. Get some Post-its, a pen, and a timer. Find a space with a blank wall (or your fridge) and set an alarm for ten or fifteen minutes. Scribble a wish or a goal on your Post-it, then run to your wall and slam the note in place. Repeat until the timer goes off. You can challenge each other to see who can get the most Post-its within the time frame, or you can just enjoy the energy of moving around and freeing yourself from overanalyzing.

Chapter 25

SPENDING FOR JOY

n part 1, you learned about the three pillars of holistic wealth building. Now it's time to delve into what each of those pillars looks like in real life.

Joy is first, and it's first for a reason. Joy isn't incidental to how you spend your money. It's not a by-product or a fringe benefit. It is a *pillar*. When we talk about building holistic wealth, this means that every step in building that wealth should feel light, easy, enjoyable, and fun, whether it's managing your money practice, designing your dream life, or buying something new. Your money needs to be spent toward joy because the feeling is a prerequisite to building wealth in that holistic, sustainable, and, of course, enjoyable way. If you aren't spending in a way that brings you joy, you aren't fully engaged in holistic wealth building.

By now, I hope you agree that you deserve to enjoy your life, both right now and for the entirety of your time on earth. You also know that money shapes and supports every aspect of your life. The clothes you wear, the house you live in, the car you drive. How much you work, how many children you have, how much time you can spend with your family and friends, how many hours a day you spend on chores. All those things cost money. This means that how you make money, how much money you make, and how you spend it all impact, well, everything. Your spending shapes your life. If you want to invite in joy, learning how to spend intentionally and spend for that joy is essential.

Most of us are never really taught how to spend money effectively. If anything, we're taught *not* to spend it, and that's that. So, as you translated your life vision into goals with financial milestones, it might have stirred something up in you. If you found yourself wanting nice things, or aspiring to wealth and abundance, you might even have felt shame bubble up. These attitudes are not always easy to shed. But I want you to make spending for joy a priority, not an afterthought.

Remember, money exists to make your life better. In fact, studies have shown that when you spend on experiences or items that you truly value, it can increase your overall happiness. You get the most value out of your money when you align your spending with what matters to you—so spending as little as possible (unless there's a material need to do so) will summon less joy than you *could* have otherwise. If you're not spending for joy, you're not getting your money's worth out of life.

Joy is the key to long-term success that most people overlook. Joy is the difference between having a full, rich life and letting the journey pass you by. As you dig into what you will be spending your money on, what will become part of your spending plan, and what you'll focus on first, I want to introduce you to the idea of "money rocks," which we touched on briefly in the introductory glossary on page xxviii. I've found that this is a simple, straightforward way to make the process of prioritizing clear and visual.

Here's the basic idea. Imagine you have a gigantic glass jar and a bunch of rocks. You're trying to fill the jar with as many rocks as possible, and in theory you can fit them all. But the rocks aren't all the same size. Some are big boulders, some are heavy stones, and some are tiny pebbles.

If you start by pouring in all the pebbles, yes, you might fit every one, but you won't have enough room for a boulder, or even a medium rock. Sure, there might still be empty space where the pebbles didn't quite fit together, but if that space is too small for a rock or a boulder, the result is that you accommodate fewer rocks *overall*. However, if you start with the boulders, then the rocks, *then* all the pebbles, you'll use the space in the jar much more efficiently.

Prioritizing your spending works in the same way. The jar you're filling is your spending plan, and you have three different sizes of rocks to fill it with. These are your money boulders, money rocks, and money pebbles.

Money boulders are the areas of your finances that could have serious negative consequences if you do *not* prioritize them. These are your basic living expenses: food, shelter, utilities, and anything that you need to do to maintain your job so that you have an income. Your boulders also include parts of your financial safety net, such as insurance and your emergency fund, as well as your retirement fund.

Next up are your money rocks. These are smaller than boulders, but still sizable. These are the categories of spending that help facilitate the life you want, and can include both financial and life goals. Not keeping up with them won't have severe consequences, but your life might be more stressful or less enjoyable. This might be a house cleaner every week or a monthly massage or a membership to a yoga studio.

Last, you have your money pebbles. These are spending categories where there's little to no negative consequence for giving them up, and where you're most willing to cut back if you need to. They include anything that's "nice to have" but is a no-brainer to pare back if it's preventing you from fitting in a money rock or boulder. Maybe you love shopping for new books, but you'd be just fine getting them from the library or subscribing to an unlimited reading app if you had to give up your one-hardcover-a-week habit. Or perhaps your favorite coffee is the locally roasted whole-bean brand, but switching to a cheaper, less gourmet blend wouldn't give you much pause.

The key to spending for joy is recognizing that *you define your own rocks.* The same expense or spending category could be a pebble for one person and a rock for someone else. Outside of the expenses that cover our basic needs, what makes a rock versus a pebble versus a boulder is up to the individual's values. There's no right or wrong answer. Even the things that are traditionally thought of as "luxuries" can be rocks, or even boulders. Maybe you're a professional cosmetician and need to show up to work in a full face of makeup every day, so makeup is a nonnegotiable boulder. Or maybe you're an office worker who just feels her most confident with foundation and mascara on; it's not necessarily a boulder, but spending at Sephora brings you more joy than any other shopping spree would, and wouldn't be the first thing to go if you needed to cut back.

Your money rocks can and will change with time. Buying diapers wasn't even a grain of sand in your spending plan before, but once you have a little one, suddenly it's a boulder. Day-care expenses are another boulder that you might have to add after you have a child, but once they start school, you get to pull that boulder out and replace it with other fun things. Moving in with a partner might shrink the size of your rent rock, while leaving roommates behind for a studio apartment might increase it.

What matters is that filling your jar takes strategy. You know the jar is a certain size, and you know what rocks you have on hand. It's up to you to use the space as efficiently as possible, getting as much meaning and safety and *joy* out of your money as possible. It's not about shrinking that jar smaller and smaller so that you have the teeniest, tiniest number of money rocks.

When we aren't taught how to spend for joy, we're being told to get a smaller jar or to leave as much empty space as possible. We learn to think of money in a way that doesn't make sense when you consider what money *is*. If it's never okay to spend, then everyone's going to feel shame when they do, because, again, *everyone uses money*. Even when you buy something you really want, you might think of it as a splurge and feel bad for picking it up. You spent for joy but stamped the joy out before you could experience it. More frequently, you may end up purchasing a substitute that feels like a "better deal" because it was less expensive. You get used to the constant deprivation and the constant settling, and find less joy, utility, and value for every dollar you spend. Because you didn't actually want that thing, you wanted this other thing over there. As with so much of your money practice, self-knowledge makes all the difference.

Our society's constant push to save can drive some people to extreme frugality, and to saving more than they need in order to meet their short- or long-term goals. It's like the only acceptable use of money is stashing it away. But spending the least has a cost of its own. It costs you experiences you would have had otherwise. It costs you opportunities and moments. It buys you regrets.

Maybe you worry that spending for joy is a slippery slope, and that if you prioritize purchasing things you want but don't technically "need," you'll lose all control. But, as with food or anything else, it's excessive restriction that can lead to control issues. Your willpower can only last so long, and we can only live with so many "nos" before we slingshot back to the other side.

This approach doesn't just make your life smaller. I see it as a constant source of tension among romantic partners. Figuring out how to fill a jar on your own is one thing, but make it a team exercise and it gets tense. You're each bringing your own money rocks. If both parties don't recognize that spending for joy is a major purpose of money, friction ensues. If you both don't recognize that spending for joy looks different for different people, it can be nearly impossible to get on the same page. That's not to say that you need to make the same decisions or engage with how you spend in the same way. It's about knowing that you can each spend for joy in your own way and still come together to hit other big financial and life goals.

When you learn how to spend for joy, you're able to create a wealth plan that aligns with your long-term vision. You're going to be able to *sustain* those goals, too, because the journey to achieving them feels fun and light instead of punishing. You're able to sustain your habits because they become easy. You're not sacrificing everything just to see that number tick up in your savings account. Life looks and feels exactly the way you want it to. And you're not worried that you're wasting money, either. You're secure in knowing that your funds are going toward your most meaningful goals. You're taking exactly the actions you intend to in making that future a reality.

Remember, your money exists to serve you. Your rocks are there to fill up your jar. A jar that's half-full or too small will make *you* feel half-full and small. Instead, let yourself be abundant with the good things you want, and feel joy in having them. Tell yourself that this is the amount you need to live, this is the amount you want to save, and you are free to do whatever you want with the rest.

Action Step

Imagine you have zero expenses, zero bills, zero obligations to spend on. You are starting over from scratch. Dump all the money rocks out of your jar. Which rocks would you put back in again? What do you actually want? What could you let go of? What would you add more of to bring more joy into your life?

Chapter 26

SPENDING FOR STABILITY

Life is filled with unexpected events. Some are pleasant surprises while others are hardships that can vary from mild annoyances to massive upheavals that change everything about what our lives look like from that moment on. Some things we can see coming and we just don't know when—I call those the expected unexpected. Things like needing a car repair or having a pipe burst in a wall. And the more you plan for them, the better you're able to weather those inevitable upheavals. This is why achieving stability is such an excellent, fundamental use of your money. To be clear, stability doesn't correspond to boredom or stagnation. It's the safety net that catches you before you hit rock bottom. It's what you get when you use your money to reduce *risk*.

Risk is a part of life. Nothing you do can ever be completely without risk. And no one can control what will happen tomorrow, which means no one can eliminate risk entirely. What you can do, though, is plan for it. Nearly every risk that might befall you is something that you can anticipate, and that means you can plan for it and build an appropriate safety net for that eventuality. Conversely, if you do not make arrangements, you'll have fewer options when the time comes. Having those safeguards in place gives future you more options. That's financial stability at work.

Take a moment to think through the kinds of risks you want to minimize. The first ones that come to mind are probably sudden and huge, right? A job loss, a major illness or disability, a natural or man-made disaster, a burglary of your house or car. These are the risks we all face at one time or another.

Those aren't the only risks you want to minimize, either. Think about the "surprise" costs that emerge, the expenses you know will pop up sooner or later. These are things like getting your leaky roof fixed, replacing appliances, or taking your car in for repairs. They're more predictable than all-out crises, because on some level, you know they're coming. But they also aren't an expense that you can plan for a specific date. You know your computer isn't going to last another twenty years, and probably not another ten. But beyond that, it gets harder to pinpoint. Does it have eight years left, or eight months? The battery might die tomorrow, or you might spill coffee on it. Or you might switch to a remote job and need to upgrade your processor. The point is, if you know it's coming, even though you don't know *when*, it should factor into your safety net.

Next, think of things that make you happy and you always want to have money to take care of. This could be your beloved pet, or your vintage Vespa, or your microbladed brows. These happy things aren't usually what you think of when you think of "risk." But they can incur spontaneous expenses, too. Your sweet little puppy eats a chicken bone and needs surgery. Your mechanic tells you to bring your scooter back in if it starts making that weird noise again. Your brows will need a touch-up someday. If you want to have the funds ready, no matter what, then you can incorporate them into your cushion, too. Remember, a safety net isn't just to keep you fed, warm, and with a roof over your head. It's to bolster and preserve the life you love. It's spending for joy, for future you.

Of course, these lists aren't exhaustive. They're a starting point to get you thinking about all the ways you'll want your financial safety net to be there for you and create stability. You'll learn more about specific parts of that safety net (like emergency funds and sinking funds) in chapter 33.

It's also impossible to come up with an exhaustive list of what your safety net can help you with, because minimizing risk will always involve some amount of speculation. You can't predict every risk that you might be exposed to in your lifetime, because you can't know precisely what will *happen* in your lifetime. Everything from a serious accident to a surprise midlife baby to a natural disaster can alter what risk might look like for you.

None of this means you can't create stability. While you may not be able to predict the future, you do have control of what you do with your money now, including how much of your income you put toward building that safety net. Treat the money you put into your safety net as a regular expense you aim to cover every single month, just like a utility bill or a housing payment. As always, remember that the most important thing is to start wherever you can so that you can build the practice of prioritizing using your money in this way. Every dollar you put in an emergency fund or sinking fund or any part of your safety net grows your financial stability, making it that much easier to navigate whatever the future holds.

Chapter 27

SPENDING FOR FREEDOM

I f stability is the confidence to know that you can weather the bad, freedom is the confidence that you can pursue the good.

Freedom is part of your life vision because your life vision is *yours.* You call the shots and make the choices. You have options. You are free to do what you want, when you want to, and your money makes it possible.

The amount you need to achieve that freedom is your *financial freedom number.* That number represents the total you'll rely on when you decide to stop working. Just as everyone's vision of a rich life is different, the cost of each rich life will be different, too. Freedom doesn't mean the same thing to all of us. Everything from where you're going to live, how many people are going to live with you, whether you have kids who are going to support you or grandkids you want to spoil, and whether you want to travel (and how often, and to where) will alter that bottom line.

Even two people with the same set of goals and standards of living can end up with a distinct financial freedom number. A person with a significant pension to support them might need $1 million to support their desired lifestyle in retirement, while their neighbor at the sixty-five-and-up community might need double that to maintain a similar lifestyle. Many people also have access to government-sponsored plans like Social Security that provide a certain amount of guaranteed income once you reach a certain age, and that's a factor, too.

The financial freedom number represents the biggest financial goal that most of us will ever face. But *biggest* doesn't have to mean *hardest*. In fact, the nature of your financial freedom number means that the money you put toward this goal will start doing some of the work *for* you as soon as you invest it.

Biggest also doesn't mean *most complicated*. This money-making-money at work in your nest egg is all thanks to the magic of compounding and the time value of money, two concepts that we discussed earlier. This means that even small amounts can add up to huge gains over time, without your having to do anything more than commit to contributing regularly.

What *biggest* does mean, beyond the sheer dollar amount, is *high priority*. The sooner you plan and take action—even imperfect action—toward growing your savings, the better off you'll be. It doesn't matter whether you have a portfolio already or you've never saved a dollar toward retirement in your life—as long as you're committed to paying yourself first, growing your wealth, and diving in, you're on the right track. This isn't just because you'll be harnessing that much more of the time value of money, though; you'll be flexing those saving muscles, too. Building strong financial habits takes time and conscious effort, but the sooner you get started, the faster those muscles can become a part of who you are.

This is where your minimum investing rate comes into play. Your minimum investing rate is the amount that you need to be investing every month in order to achieve your financial freedom number on the timeline that you desire. It's what cultivates true, lifelong freedom—not just because it's building the nest egg that will ensure you can retire in the comfortable lifestyle of your choosing, but because when you hit that minimum investing rate every month, you get a feeling of freedom now. It's beginning with the end in mind all over again.

Now, you might assume that because this number is so significant and such a high priority, you should just put as much money toward it as you possibly can. The problem there is that it gets you away from specifics. You need to know your financial freedom number for the same reason you need to know your long-term life goals: It's critical to identify your target to make progress in that direction. It's kind of like golf. Now, I've never played golf, and I've watched it only a few times, but every time I see someone on TV sinking a hole in one or even just hitting the green, I wonder how it's even possible. It's not so much the distance that's impressive, but the accuracy. Golf isn't scored just on how far you can hit the ball: smacking it three hundred yards in the wrong direction is worse than whiffing it, because you've wasted a stroke and made it *much* trickier to come in under par. To become really great at golf, you have to always laser in on that little flag and aim directly for it.

Maybe that analogy got away from me, but the point is that you want to make sure all your strokes are getting you closer to the hole—your financial freedom number. Your minimum investing rate is like a swing of the club that's accurate, confident, and relaxed instead of all over the place. It's what moves you steadily toward your goal and frees you from feeling obligated to put away "as much as possible," because you know you're on track.

As you read the next section, remember that all the numbers we'll be discussing, from your net worth to your minimum investing rate, are the tools that will help you build your best life. Start where you can today. You deserve that dream life, and you have what it takes to achieve it.

Now that you're buzzing with excitement over the life your money will create, let's dive into the money practice that you'll use to make it happen.

PART 5

CREATE YOUR MONEY PRACTICE

Chapter 28

YOUR MONEY PRACTICE

By now, you understand what money is. You know that there are seven money capacities that you need to foster. You have explored what having a rich life means to you, now and in the future. You've taken a few action steps, too.

Let's build on that positive momentum with more action. It's time to create your money practice.

Your money practice is the series of actions you take regularly to manage your finances and make them grow. It's a set of steps that you commit to on a routine basis to stay on track with your goals.

Everyone's money practice will look different for the reasons we touched on in the last section: Your goals and desired lifestyle won't be exactly the same as someone else's, and neither will your income. No one-size-fits-all practice would be nearly as effective as the one you are able to cultivate with a little guidance and practice. Your money practice is a muscle that gets stronger and more capable of executing moves with ease the more you use it. With the guidance of the financial principles you'll find in this part, you will feel competent and confident in your own ability to create a financial practice that supports your financial and life goals for the rest of your life.

You're already in tune with what you want your money to do for you. This section will help you develop, calibrate, and use the tools that will make it happen. However, there are certain things that everyone should include in their money practice, such as knowing your numbers, creating a one-year spending plan, tracking your spending, and so on. But they're also flexible, and once you understand the setup, you can customize and tweak however it makes sense to you.

Remember, practice means practice, not perfection. Practice is about doing something again and again, fine-tuning as you go and figuring out what works. It's also something you keep up, no matter what, even as your mastery grows. The legendary cellist Yo-Yo Ma is considered one of the most talented and influential musicians of all time, and he still practices up to six hours every day. There is always more to learn and do. There is always room for improvement. Practice lets you grow and keeps you in touch with all the progress you've made.

Having a money practice is saying, "I am continuously using my money to create the life that I want." But instead of merely saying it, you're doing it. You're living it. You're taking action. And *that* is what creates that life for you.

So let's get started.

Chapter 29

KNOW YOUR NUMBERS

W e've spent time getting to know what you want your money to do for you. Now we're going to look at what your money is doing. By looking at the current state of your finances, we can chart the path from where you are right now to where you want to go.

Depending on what you've done in the past for money management, looking at your numbers and checking in on them on a regular basis might be new to you. This chapter is your invitation to step into that as a practice. Knowing your numbers gives you a clear picture of your finances so you can act with intention. That clarity brings a sense of empowerment. When you don't know what's going on with your money, it's like trying to find your way out of a huge, pitch-black room. Even if you know there's an exit door, you can't know for sure which direction to walk in until you know where you are. Knowing your numbers throws on the floodlights and lets you see everything—including the quickest route to where you want to go.

The primary numbers you'll be looking at are your cash flow and your net worth. These particular numbers are like snapshots: They capture the state of things in one moment in time and provide insight into the full landscape of your financial life. And not to worry— while you'll pull together a decent amount of information to calculate these numbers, the math itself is simple.

Both your annual cash flow number and your net worth number establish a baseline for where you are now. Your cash flow will help you see where your funds are going and decide where you want them to go from here on out, while your net worth will help you see your overall balance of wealth versus debt and provide a starting point for your wealth-building strategy. The way your life looks from day to day is a direct result of how you choose to earn money and how you choose to spend it. Cash flow represents the total of those choices in number form. The way you'll strategize in your journey depends on where you're starting, and that's what your net worth tells you. Understanding both is what will allow you to make specific, actionable plans to get to your ideal lifestyle.

Let's define cash flow first. Your annual cash flow measures how much money you have coming in and how much you're spending over the course of a year. (When you create your one-year spending plan in chapter 30, you'll break that amount down into a monthly number.) Looking at a full one year of cash flow lets you zoom out from a paycheck or monthly cycle to that big-picture perspective. It can also show you just how far you've come. When you compare your annual cash flow year over year, you see your small wins add up in a big way. And anything that makes your progress hit home is a win in my book.

Next up is net worth. Your net worth is the total value of all your assets (such as cash, retirement accounts, real estate, valuables, etc.) minus the total value of your debts and liabilities. While your cash flow is measured over time (a year, in this case), your net worth is a snapshot of your finances at one point in time. As such, it has its limits. Your net worth can't tell you whether you're on track to hit your financial goals or predict what's possible. It might shrink after you make decisions in the name of building wealth, like taking on debt to acquire a revenue-producing rental property. It's also subject to factors beyond your control, like market conditions. So while you generally want to see your net worth increase over time, just keep in mind that this number shows you one moment, not a trajectory or a prediction.

Now that you understand what these numbers are, it's time to figure them out for yourself.

First up: annual cash flow. Since cash flow is money in minus money out, you'll start by figuring out your income. Your income is any money that flows to you that you can spend on personal expenses. It's simple to figure out, but it's a bit more involved than just putting down your annual salary. You probably know that some money comes out of your paycheck before it gets to you (like taxes, insurance premiums, and mandatory retirement contributions). For your annual cash flow, you're interested in what's known as your *net income*, which is the amount that lands in your bank account after those deductions are taken out. Your *gross income*, by contrast, is the total amount of money you earn *before* those deductions are taken out, while net income is what's available to you, so that's the relevant figure here. However, I do think it's worth your time to figure out your gross income and total deductions, too. You likely can't reduce those deductions, but you do pay them, so in the name of awareness, it's worth knowing how much of your money goes toward them.

Start by finding your gross income. If you're an employee, then you can typically look at your paycheck stubs to find this number and multiply it by the total pay periods in the year to get your annual gross income. You can also look at your annual W-2 if your employer issued one last year. If you have an irregular income, you have a few options. If you have a business accountant or bookkeeper (for a small business or freelance work), you can ask them for a profit-and-loss sheet, which will show your annual gross revenue. You can also just add up your deposits from last year, or you can make your best guess based on how you expect this coming year to go. (If you're estimating, I recommend that you lean toward using the lower end of the range when it comes to your income and the higher end when it comes to your expenses. That way, you're looking at the worst-case scenario versus an overly optimistic version of your cash flow.)

If you have a secondary source of income, include that, too. If it's money flowing to you that you're able to spend on personal expenses, it counts toward your gross income. Typical sources include child support, real estate income, investment income, royalties, side hustles, gig work, or a year-end bonus. Things like income tax refunds or credit card rewards can vary depending on a lot of factors, so overall, it's better to leave those out and not count money before it's in your pocket, so to speak.

After you've written down your gross income, list the deductions that are taken out of your paycheck every pay period. These will vary from person to person, but might include things like taxes, insurance premiums, flexible spending or health savings account contributions, wage garnishments, or retirement or pension contributions. Basically, deductions are anything taken out before your paycheck hits your bank account, either because they're required to be or because you opted in. Again, multiply the deductions by the number of pay periods per year to get the annual numbers. If you have income from freelancing, gig work, side hustles, and so on, your taxes won't be automatically deducted, but you do still *owe* taxes on that money, which must be reported to the IRS. You can look up your federal and state tax rates to get a rough idea of what to "deduct."

Now that you have your gross annual income and your total annual deductions, the math is simple. Subtract the deductions from your gross income and there you have it: your net income. Now you know exactly how much you have available to spend over the course of a year. You're halfway to your yearly cash flow.

Next up are your expenses. You'll find a checklist on page 181 outlining the general categories and the items that fall into them, which you can consult as you're thinking through these.

To figure out your cash flow, let's look at your mandatory expenses, which cover all the things you couldn't survive without. You might have heard these called *fixed* expenses, but I find this term to be misleading or confusing, since it could suggest that the *amount* of the expense is fixed (as in a *fixed income*). In reality, any expense can change with time or effort, so to keep that top of mind, I call them *mandatory* instead. Regardless, a mandatory (or fixed) expense is something you're required to pay to keep yourself going. This includes rent or mortgage, required debt payments, the electric bill, the gas you need to put in your car so that you can get to your job and run necessary errands, your car insurance, childcare so that you can work, and so on. It also includes basic grocery expenses and basic household items, because you need to eat, brush your teeth, and wash your clothes as a part of daily life.

Look at your mandatory expenses and add them up, using the categories as a guide. Keep in mind that this process is all about getting you in tune with the full scope of your finances, so your objective here is to make the best guess you can. Don't feel obligated to go through last year's bank statements to get this number down to the penny. You can group similar expenses to keep things simple (for example, car registration, oil changes, and car washes all fit under the category of "car maintenance"). You'll get into the specifics when you create your one-year spending plan, but broad strokes are fine for now.

Now that you know your net income and your mandatory expenses, you can calculate your annual budget surplus. Your budget surplus is the amount available after covering the necessities. It's the money that will help you meet your financial and life goals and the money you'll have available for discretionary spending. Again, the math is straightforward: Subtract your total mandatory expenses from your net income. Write down the number: voilà, budget surplus. Don't fixate on the amount for the time being; you'll come back to it later on. For now, give yourself a pat on the back for doing the work to know this key figure in your financial life.

One number down, and one to go. Net worth is equally simple to determine. Again, it's a subtraction problem, except in this case, you're subtracting your liabilities (the total amount you owe) from your assets (the total value of all that you own). And, again, you'll start by adding up the "positive" side of the equation.

An asset is anything that is held in cash or has value and could be sold for cash. To find the total value of your assets, start by listing them all. The major assets you should include in your asset list are houses, cars, boats, stocks and real estate investments, and the cash value of pensions and cash value of insurance policies. Beyond those major assets, it's up to you what else you include. For example, you might exclude money that's earmarked for a particular expense, like your child's college savings account, or the cash in your checking account dedicated to expenses for the coming month. You might want to include the fair market values of assets like jewelry, art, furniture, and the like, or you might not. There's no right or wrong here, because this net worth number is for *you* to gain awareness. You don't have to include every single asset on your net worth tracker for it to be a useful resource. Make a judgment call based on where you want insight, and lean into your role as the decision maker in your financial life.

The one thing you do need is consistency. If you include one asset, include all your assets in that category. If you have an asset with corresponding debt, such as a computer you financed, be sure to include its resale value as well. Otherwise, your net worth won't be balanced, because that debt will be going in your liability section.

After you've listed your assets, add up the total value. Bank accounts and financial assets (like retirement or investment accounts) already have a dollar figure attached. When it comes to nonfinancial assets, internet searches are your best friend. Research the going rate for similar cars or similar houses in your local market and use that to make an educated estimate of fair market value. Keep in mind that this net worth calculation is just a tracking tool; it's not meant to be perfectly accurate, and no one's going to audit you. A good guess works perfectly well for your purposes.

Now that you've listed your assets, you'll do the same for liabilities. Write down all debts that you owe and their current balances. These will be things like student loans, car loans, mortgages, credit card balances, 401(k) loans, home equity loans, and personal loans. Debts that don't have an outstanding balance, like a credit card you pay off in full every month, don't have to be included here. Debts that you aren't actively paying but still owe a balance on, such as a medical bill that's in collections, or student loans in temporary forbearance, *should* be on your list, however. Also list any debts that you're paying as wage garnishments (such as tax arrears or child support arrears—though not normal child support payments, because those are expenses, not liabilities).

Now that you've listed your assets and liabilities, the only thing left to do is to add up the total for each. Then subtract your total liabilities from your total assets to get your net worth.

You did it. Congratulations! You know those two critical numbers: your yearly cash flow and your net worth. That's a huge step, and not a small amount of work, so you should feel amazing about the time and effort you put in.

As you look at this overview of your finances, a lot of feelings and conclusions may come up in your mind. Take a moment to sit with your numbers and reflect on how you feel about them. Did any of the amounts surprise you? Are there any areas where you'd like to reduce your spending? Are there areas where you'd like to increase your spending? How do you feel about your income and your budget surplus? Set aside fifteen to thirty minutes to journal about these questions. Write them down, sort them out, and reframe them if necessary. You can go back to part 2, on money stories, if you need a refresher to determine facts from thoughts.

Remember that your numbers are just a snapshot of one moment in your overall journey. They're a picture of where you are right now, and where you are right now isn't where you'll be a month from now, a year from now, or five years from now.

Your numbers don't affect whether you're on the road to success. But the fact that you put in the time to know them does. Your actions and decisions shape your financial future. You've taken the necessary steps to know what you're working with. You're that much better equipped to make clear financial decisions. You're that much closer to getting your money to serve the best version of your life, now and in the future.

EXPENSE CATEGORIES CHECKLIST

Use this list to help put together your mandatory and discretionary expenses when calculating your cash flow. You don't need to include all of these, since some obviously will not apply to you and your situation, and you can combine or split categories however makes sense and feels clear to you. This list is here to jog your thinking and give you a jumping-off point.

Mandatory Expenses

Housing:

- ☐ Mortgage or rent
- ☐ Homeowner's or renter's insurance
- ☐ Property taxes
- ☐ HOA fees
- ☐ Home and yard maintenance

Utilities:

- ☐ Electricity
- ☐ Gas
- ☐ Water
- ☐ Sewer
- ☐ Internet
- ☐ Phone
- ☐ Trash and recycling

Lifestyle:

- ☐ Groceries
- ☐ Clothing
- ☐ Household goods
- ☐ Hygiene and personal care items
- ☐ Childcare/child support
- ☐ Baby/child supplies

Insurance:

- ☐ Health insurance
- ☐ Dental insurance
- ☐ Vision insurance
- ☐ Umbrella insurance
- ☐ Short-/long-term disability insurance

Medical:

☐ Copays and out-of-pocket costs

☐ Medications

☐ Medical devices and supplies

Transportation:

☐ Car payment

☐ Gas

☐ Car insurance

☐ Parking fees

☐ Car maintenance

☐ Transit passes

Pets:

☐ Pet food and supplies

☐ Vet visits

☐ Pet medications

Discretionary Expenses

Home:

☐ Home decor

☐ Home renovations

☐ Domestic services (housekeeper, lawn service, pest control, etc.)

☐ Electronics/devices

Entertainment:

☐ Eating out/takeout

☐ Books and magazines

☐ Cable/streaming services

☐ Events (concerts, movies, sports games, etc.)

☐ Memberships (online communities, sports clubs, etc.)

☐ Hobbies

Personal Care:

- [ ] Haircuts and hair styling
- [ ] Makeup
- [ ] Beauty services (nails, waxing, facials, etc.)
- [ ] Massages
- [ ] Gym membership

Travel:

- [ ] Airfare/train fare
- [ ] Lodging
- [ ] Dining
- [ ] Transportation (car rental, transit, tour bus, etc.)
- [ ] Admission fees (amusement parks, museums, etc.)

Children:

- [ ] Tutoring/private lessons
- [ ] Sports and activities
- [ ] Allowance

Pets:

- [ ] Pet insurance
- [ ] Pet sitting/walking/daycare

Gifts and Giving:

- [ ] Gifts (birthday, holiday, etc.)
- [ ] Nonprofit/political donations
- [ ] Tithing or stewardship

Chapter 30

CREATE YOUR ONE-YEAR SPENDING PLAN

Let's talk about a different kind of numbers now. You know how computer code is a series of zeros and ones that would look indecipherable to most of us, but the result is something a layperson can make sense of? When you pull up Instagram, you just see cute selfies and dog pictures. You don't see strings of binary or falling green numbers like in *The Matrix*. But you still understand that somewhere in your phone, there's a bunch of ones and zeros making that social media magic happen, bringing you what you want, when you want it.

Your one-year spending plan is the zeros and ones of your life. It's what makes the life you want possible. It's your decisions and goals mapped out. It's how you can use your money to change what your life looks like, both now and in the future. When you take control of those numbers, you seize the power to shape your future.

And that's amazing.

The one-year spending plan is a budget, but it's also more than a budget. It's about creating possibility in a real way, starting from the snapshot of where you are and aiming for the snapshot of where you want to go. It builds on the empowerment of knowing your numbers and gives you a plan to take action.

Here's the process in a nutshell. First, you'll add in your after-tax income from each of your income sources. Then you'll total up your income for the month and add your mandatory expenses, grouped by category to keep things organized. Then you'll add in your monthly debt payments. Add up the mandatory expenses and debt payments (because debt payments are expenses) and subtract that from your after-tax income. That number is your budget surplus, and that's what you get to allocate to all your financial goals, life goals, and discretionary spending.

Before you make your plan, however, you'll want a picture of how you're spending right now. Your goal is to make your spending plan as true to life as possible, and in order to do that, you need a baseline sense of your current monthly spending. The good news is that you've done quite a bit of the legwork already, since you pulled together your income and mandatory expenses when you created your annual cash flow. What you'll need to gather now are your debt payments and discretionary expenses. For your debt payments, list the name of the debt, the type of debt, the due date, the interest rate, and your minimum monthly payment. (It's true that debts are technically expenses, but since they come with a different set of considerations, like the interest you're paying, it's worth separating them out. Laying them out here will also save you time when creating your debt payoff plan in chapter 32.)

Next, write out your lifestyle and discretionary expenses. These include anything nonessential, such as eating out, gym memberships, personal grooming, cable, extracurricular activities for your kids, gifts, and so on. If your life were an ice-cream sundae, these are the sprinkles and cherry on top. They make your sundae extra special, but if you took some (or all) of them away, you'd still have ice cream.

You might notice your discretionary expenses are a bit more work to categorize and add up. That's normal. Most people underestimate just how much they tend to spend on the fun stuff. This is especially true if they're using cash, because there are no card transactions to refresh their memory. Do your best and be as accurate as you can. Look back over bank statements to start. If you order a lot online (Amazon Prime, anyone?) then log into your account and get your order history so you can divide your purchases into the appropriate categories. If you end up with a "miscellaneous discretionary spending" group, that's fine. At the very least, you know you spent that money on something that wasn't a mandatory expense or debt. And as you start tracking your spending as a habit, you'll have an easier time with this.

Before you move on to the one-year spending plan, take a moment to look at your monthly spending habits. Did you get big value from your big discretionary expenses? Or did you maybe get more value from categories you spent less in? Are there changes you might want to make when you lay out your spending plan? Getting a general sense of your priorities and values alongside these numbers can help kick-start your planning.

Now, it's time to make the spending plan itself. The basic setup of any one-year spending plan is a sheet that's thirteen columns across (one column to list expense categories, and then one for each month of the year) and as many rows deep as it needs to be to accommodate all your costs. You can make your spending plan with pen and paper, but I recommend placing it in a spreadsheet instead. Paper budget planners are popular these days, but they're time intensive, too, and you're more likely to end up with a calculation error. Start in the January column. (Once this column is done, you'll copy it over to fill out the rest of the year). First, list each of your income sources, giving each its own row, and the amount it brings in monthly. Remember, we're looking at net income here, but you have all those paycheck deductions tracked in your yearly cash flow for your reference.

If you're not paid monthly, you have a few options. You can calculate your annual income and divide it by 12. If you're paid weekly, you can multiply your weekly paycheck amount by 52, and then divide by 12. Or you can budget using your minimum monthly pay frequency, adding in the extra paychecks where they fall in your calendar. If you're paid biweekly, budget for two paychecks a month, add the other two paychecks wherever they fall in the calendar. If you're paid less frequently than once a month, calculate your annual after-tax income, then divide that by 12 to get your monthly amount.

If you have an irregular or variable income, use a modified version of the strategy for people who are paid less frequently than monthly. Calculate your annual after-tax income, then divide by 12. Even though you won't make exactly that amount each month, it'll generate a sort of DIY regular pay schedule. When you have a high-income month, transfer everything above what you'll need to meet that month's expenses into a savings account. When you have a low-income month, use that cushion to bring you up to your average monthly income. Alternatively, you can be conservative and simply set up your annual budget using your lowest monthly income as a base, then adjust in those months where you end up making more.

Next, add in your mandatory expenses by category to keep things nice and organized. You can also pull the same categories you used to calculate your annual cash flow. Some of your mandatory expenses might fluctuate depending on usage, such as your electric bill, so I suggest using an average-to-high amount based on past bills to make sure that every expense will be covered. For expenses that are regular, but less frequent than monthly, like a quarterly HOA fee, you can either add them to the month they'll be due, or add up the total amount for the year and divide by 12 to factor this cost into each month's budget.

Next, add in debts. Not all debts have to go in this section: For example, your mortgage might be in your Housing category, or your car payment in Transportation. Again, do what makes sense to you and gives you the most clarity at a glance. It's all about figuring out a system that feels intuitive, because that's the system that'll be easiest to stick to.

After all your debts and mandatory expenses are in, it's time to calculate your monthly budget surplus. Subtract your debts and your mandatory expenses from your income. The amount left over is your budget surplus, or the amount you have to spend on discretionary expenses.

If Your Monthly Spending Leaves You in the Negative

Hopefully, your current spending leaves you with a positive budget surplus at the end of each month. If that's not the case, however, don't worry. You're not alone. Right now, you're spending more than you bring in, meaning you don't have enough income to cover your monthly expenses. This shortfall is called a budget deficit, and there are plenty of strategies that you can use to tackle it, including:

- Look for ways to cut or reduce your expenses in the short term. Prioritize paying the spending that you need to keep your housing, employment, and assets. Anything discretionary that you're not truly enjoying or not using is something you can eliminate.

- Work to grow your income both at your day job and with a side hustle or business.

- Explore strategies to help you reduce the impact of your debt on your budget.

- Consider reaching out to a lawyer or other financial advisor who can act as your fiduciary (meaning that they work based on your best interests, not how much money they'll make from you). They can create a custom plan to help you negotiate with your creditors, or pursue bankruptcy if that's the best option.

- If your budget deficit stems from having too much debt, there are options here, too. Start by reaching out to your creditors to negotiate a lower interest rate or repayment terms that you're able to meet. Many lenders are open to working with customers, so it's worth having the conversation. Another strategy is to consolidate high-interest debt into a lower-interest loan. If you choose this route, you're going to want to make sure that you completely understand the terms of the loan, that it isn't structured in a way that will actually cost you more than your current debts, and that the company that you're working with is reputable. A third option to consider is filing for bankruptcy. If your situation warrants it, consider contacting an attorney or a financial advisor who can act as a fiduciary and help you decide on your best course of action for your situation.

A budget deficit is a challenging bind to find yourself in, but it's just a temporary one. Think of it as a short period that you're working your way through on your path to building wealth and creating the life that you want.

With your budget surplus calculated, add in your discretionary expenses. Most likely, you'll want to have a mix of lifestyle spending, saving, and perhaps some amount of extra debt payoff. Remember your money rocks and spending for joy as you allocate, and look at your current spending as a jumping-off point.

When your discretionary expenses are done, you've finished your first month. Now just copy the numbers in your January column over to the rest of the months in the year. Then take a moment to look at the year as a whole and make sure you've included everything.

Feel free to customize your spending plan setup with whatever other information might be helpful. For example, you might want to add a column with the due date for each bill. You could also consider tracking your total debt balance in separate rows beneath each monthly debt payment. And as you track and reconcile your spending, add columns to note down your actual spending alongside the plan. Most likely, you'll realize what you want to add or adjust in the setup as you start using it and start spending. That's all part of the process.

Chapter 31

TRACK YOUR SPENDING AND RECONCILE YOUR BUDGET

This chapter is all about *budget* (the verb). You just created your *budget* (the noun) when you made your one-year spending plan. *Budget* the noun is what helped you figure out your income and expenses, and then decide what you want to spend your money on going forward.

But as a money practice, you're interested in *budget* the verb. You're all about taking action. *Budget* the verb is when you track how closely you stick to your plan and then adjust as you go. It's the active part of budgeting, the thing that you do and practice regularly as opposed to the thing you put together in a single session. See? Budget is a thing you make and a thing you do. Noun *and* verb.

The point is, budgeting as a money practice is a three-part process. You plan, you execute, and you tweak. You did the first part when making your spending plan. Now it's time to execute and tweak. Executing your plan means tracking your spending, aka looking at how closely you followed the plan you laid out. Tweaking is when you look at the plan, look at the actual spending you tracked, and decide whether you want to make any adjustments.

Let's start with how you're going to track your expenses. There are many ways to do this, but as always, remember that there's no *best* way. There's only the way that's best for you. Whichever way makes sense, feels easy, and you can envision sticking with as a practice is the right path.

One tracking option is to use cash for everything. Many people enjoy the "cash envelope" system because it's straightforward and simple. At the beginning of each month, you look at your total planned spending and pull out that amount of cash from your bank account. You then separate that cash into envelopes that match the categories in your budget, with each holding exactly the amount you plan to spend in that category. Cash envelopes are equal parts tracking system and accountability system. When you're first starting, you might need this level of accountability. Or you might just like that it makes your money feel *real* because you're holding it in your hand.

Another option is a sort of virtual envelope system. In this system, all expenses are paid from a single checking account. For savings goals, you use multiple accounts to separate your money by category. If you use credit cards, you'll have one credit card and personal checking account for personal discretionary spending (and if you have a partner, you'll each have your own card and checking account), and another for general spending.

Third, you can track your spending right in your spending plan spreadsheet. There are several ways to do this. You can add a column next to each month, then use that column to note your spending. That way, they're side by side and easy to compare. Alternatively, you could make a second copy of your one-year spending plan and adjust the numbers right in the spreadsheet. Or you could create separate spreadsheets for each month, which allows you to go into more detail.

Last, you can reconcile your spending by using free apps or with plain old pen and paper. Again, there's no right choice here. Go with your gut, try them all out, and see which one you like the best, or make up your own system.

No matter what, you will always have to spend some amount of time looking at your finances. As you get used to your system, you'll dial in your spending plan and largely put your finances on autopilot so that it takes you very little time to reconcile and update your budget. But life happens, and it's inevitable that unexpected things will come up, whether it's a burst pipe or an impromptu dinner with friends. Yes, these things will throw you off a bit, but your spending plan is meant to be flexible. It's supposed to change as your needs change. At the same time, it's a balance. If you always allow your wants to push out your needs, like saving for retirement, then you'll slow your financial progress over time. You might have to say no a lot more often because you don't have as many choices available. Finding that balance means understanding the impact that your choices will have on the rest of your year and proceeding accordingly.

Chapter 32

MANAGE DEBT

You've read a lot about debt in this book so far, and now it's time to get into more of the nuts and bolts of managing your debt as part of your money practice.

Managing debt effectively isn't just about debt payoff. It's about using debt in a way that helps create the life you want both now and in the future. When you have a solid debt strategy in place, you'll feel completely in control. You will understand it and know exactly how it fits your overall financial strategy.

From now on, before you take on any new debt, you'll make sure that you think through a repayment plan for it. That way, you'll know exactly how much the debt will cost you, how you'll repay it, and the impact it will have on your wealth-building journey.

Your goal here is to decrease your reliance on debt over time. But not because debt is bad. Debt isn't bad, as you now know. Debt is a financial tool that you can use to build your best life. When used effectively, it can help you build wealth faster and give you more convenience and flexibility in when and how you make purchases. But it's a tool that works best when you consciously choose to use it, and to make a conscious and educated choice, you need to have multiple options. When you *rely* on debt, it's your only option. Sometimes it's your last resort. And when you have only one option, you don't really have a choice at all.

When you decrease your reliance on debt, however, your options open back up. You have the power to choose how to make purchases and build wealth. Sometimes that choice will be to take on debt. Sometimes that choice will be to use cash. The point is, you get to choose.

Managing your debt effectively does not mean that debt payoff is your most important financial priority. It doesn't even mean paying it off as soon as possible, either. It's about opening your options and making conscious choices.

Before moving on to building a strategy, there's one thing I want to encourage you to do. Stop taking on more debt until you have a repayment strategy in place. Taking on more debt will likely increase your monthly expenses, potentially causing you to have to compromise your other financial goals. It will turn your debt into a moving target and make it harder for you to build the habits that will keep you out of unexpected debt in the future. Once you have a repayment plan, then you can weigh the pros and cons of taking on additional debt, and work that into your spending and repayment strategy. But for now, stick with shaping your plan around the debt you currently have.

The first step in managing your debt is knowing your debt. Many people haven't put in the time to fully understand what's going on with their finances, and this is especially true when it comes to debt.

I definitely didn't understand debt when I first started out. I got my first credit card when I was sixteen. I didn't know that sixteen-year-olds can't legally *have* credit cards. I used to walk home from the train across a college campus near my high school, and one day I came across a credit card company doing a classic T-shirt-and-water-bottle giveaway for any students who filled out an application. I didn't understand the details, but I filled out my form, got my freebies, and a few weeks later, my new credit card came in the mail. It had my name on it, and gave me up to $500 to spend. I was excited. It was free money, as far as I knew. I used that card to buy McDonald's and clothes and other things my sixteen-year-old self wanted until "Declined" finally popped up. At that point, I figured I'd used it up somehow and that was that. I didn't give it another thought, and I certainly didn't pay it. Even three years later, when my mom forwarded me a bill that had arrived at the house, I still didn't understand what I was supposed to do. It wasn't until I was trying to buy a house three years later that I learned I needed to pay this bill off. It turned out it was *not* free money after all.

However, while my really-not-thought-through first credit card experience almost stopped me from getting my first house, being conscious and purposeful with debt allowed me to get a law degree. I took out much more in student loans than I charged on that first credit card. The difference was that I took on the student loans intentionally and understood exactly how they would affect my life afterward and what it would take to pay them off. Yes, I did have over $160,000 in student loans, but because I had paid attention to my debt and taken the time to think it through, I understood the impact that the loans would have on my budget, so I was able to buy a home while still retiring my student loans on the schedule that I had planned out. So it's not that having debt is bad, and it's not that having more debt is worse. It's that debt that's acquired haphazardly is more likely to have an unintended negative impact on your goals, whereas debt that is acquired with purpose can actually support your goals and help you reach them faster. Knowing your debt and getting those numbers out in the open is the first step to managing it effectively.

First, list your debts. Common forms of debt include credit cards, student loans, car loans, mortgages, and personal loans, but you might have other types, like medical debt, purchase-financing plans (like for cell phones), or debts owed to family or friends. Include your student loans, too, even if they're in deferment, forbearance, or not currently in repayment.

Next, list the due date, minimum payment, interest rate, and the total interest owed on your debt. If you make the minimum payments, interest is the extra cost you pay above the original principal you borrowed. While you might have heard that interest is a waste of money, this is a thought, not a fact. Only you can decide if interest is worth it. But the only way you can make that decision is if you know exactly how much you'll be paying. Once you know what that debt is costing you, you can then make an informed decision about whether and how quickly you want to eliminate it.

Start by looking at the paper and electronic statements that you get every month. Every credit card statement must include information about your interest rate and how much interest you'll incur if you make minimum payments rather than paying it off in full every month.

Installment loans are a bit different. They typically disclose the total interest in the documents you get when you sign the loan itself. For any debt that doesn't list the total anticipated interest you'll pay, reach out to the lender and ask them, or use an online calculator to get an estimate. You'll input the total amount remaining on the principal, the interest rate, the repayment period, and the minimum monthly payment, and the calculator will add up the interest you'll pay over time.

Repeat this for each of your debts and fill in the total interest column. If a debt has a variable interest rate, either use the highest rate you expect it to reach or figure out a reasonable average based on what the rate has been in the past. As you calculate the total interest, keep in mind that these numbers don't have to be exact down to the penny. A few hundred dollars in either direction will not make a huge impact for our purposes, so don't get too granular here.

Once you've gathered your numbers, it's time to lay out your debt repayment strategy. The first order of business is to decide how much you'll pay toward your debts every month. A common myth is that if you only make the minimum debt payments, you'll never pay them off. The reality is that most debts, including credit cards, are structured in a way that will allow you to pay them off eventually, even if you're contributing just the minimum each month. But it's true that the longer you hang on to a debt, the more interest you'll accumulate.

That still doesn't necessarily mean that the "best" way to deal with it is to pay it down as quickly as possible—or as slowly as possible. The best approach is a balanced debt payoff plan. Balanced debt payoff allows you to take a more nuanced approach to debt payoff where you can retire your debt on a timeline that you're happy with while still working toward other meaningful priorities in life.

Balanced debt payoff could mean making smaller payments planned over a longer period of time. For example, if the interest rate on your car loan is low, you may decide that you are not in a rush to pay it off early because the monthly minimum payment gives you the financial flexibility to do other things. Instead of rapidly paying down that car note, you might choose to beef up your emergency fund, for example, or your retirement savings. Or you might just enjoy having the extra funds to spend on your lifestyle now. That's a trade-off that you can decide to make, because you understand what you're doing, you've planned for the expenses involved, and you've found that balance based on what your priorities are.

However, there may be instances where a balanced debt-payoff approach calls for making more or larger debt payments so that you are able to retire your debt faster. Again, it's all about finding the balance that makes sense for you, given your priorities. Maybe your lifestyle spending is at a level you're very happy with, your savings and investment accounts are on track, and you still have a nice surplus that you need to allocate in your spending plan. Paying off your debt faster lowers your overall minimum expenses and potentially allows you to save on interest.

Aside from the cost savings, there are times when you might need to lower the amount of debt you're carrying. For example, if you're getting ready to buy a house, you might want to rapidly pay a credit card balance or loan over the next few months to make it easier to qualify for a mortgage. Zeroing out an account means one less thing for the mortgage company to look at and might also boost your credit score to boot. However, prioritizing rapid debt payoff, making larger and more frequent debt payments, can also mean you could miss out on investing or neglect your emergency fund, putting yourself at unnecessary financial risk. Or it can cause you to miss out on once-in-a-lifetime moments, like traveling to a friend's destination wedding or throwing your child a graduation party, when taking a more gradual approach could have afforded you both.

Only you can judge which trade-offs make sense for you and your life. Again, the key is to make these decisions with intention and, ideally, in a way that doesn't hinder your other goals. That said, even if you're leaning toward rapid payoff, I suggest building up a three-month fund before you go all in. If a true emergency strikes, taking care of your immediate needs will be your top priority, and you'll want cash to cover those essential expenses. Debt payoff isn't more important than housing or food.

With that in mind, it's time to decide how much of your monthly budget surplus you want to allocate to repayment. That surplus, which you calculated earlier, is the money available to you every month after you've paid your mandatory expenses, including minimum payments on debt. If you divide your total debt balance by your monthly budget surplus, you can get an idea of how quickly you could pay off all your debts. For example, if you have a $1,000 monthly surplus and $150,000 in debt, then you know you could pay off your debt in approximately twelve years. This example doesn't account for interest, but it gives you a general sense of what your repayment timeline could look like.

It's up to you to decide how much of your surplus you want to allocate toward debt. It doesn't have to be the same amount each month, but you should pick a minimum you're willing to contribute and commit to that. You could also choose to put all that surplus toward debt repayment for half the year, and then take a more moderate approach for the second half. Or you could focus on paying down just a few high-interest debts at a time until they're gone—since those cost you more for each dollar that you've borrowed compared to debts that have a lower interest rate—and then slowly pay the rest.

Once you've worked out how much money will go toward debt each month, you'll want to decide which debts to prioritize paying. There's no rule of thumb here, because, again, debt payoff is part of *your* wealth-building journey and *your* life goals. Take some time to think through what both look like.

Is your highest consideration building wealth? In that case, you'll probably want to focus on paying the highest-interest debt first, then move on to the next-highest-interest debt, and so on. This approach means paying less in the long run, because you'll hold that high interest debt over shorter periods of time.

Are you trying to simplify your finances? Paying off small debts first can help you there, because every debt you pay off is one less bill to manage every month. If you want to streamline the number of payments you make, focus on eliminating smaller debts first. That said, the advantage here is really just in that streamlining. There's no special advantage beyond the time and energy you save in keeping tabs on an additional account. Paying $1,000 to knock out a small debt isn't inherently better than putting that $1,000 toward a $10,000 loan. Every dollar brings you one step closer to your financial goals and your dream life. So I encourage you not to default to paying off smaller debts first because it feels like a quick win. Remember, you're creating sustainable habits to build wealth over time, and to empower you to make the best decisions for your specific vision of your future.

Do you want to free up some extra cash and grow your monthly surplus? Consider paying off your loans with high minimum payments first. Joseph and I did this when I decided to leave my day job to run our business. We rapidly paid off some low-interest debts just so we could reduce our minimum monthly expenses. Business income isn't always predictable, especially when a business is in a massive growth phase, and a more sizable surplus in our spending plan gave us more cash to cover our expenses.

After you think through your goals, take a look at your debt list. Consider the amount of interest you pay monthly for each versus the smallest account balance for each, and decide the order in which you would like to pay them off. Then number the debts according to priority, which will represent the order in which you will apply that minimum monthly surplus to getting rid of them each month. Once you've decided where to focus, work out how much cash you'll put toward those debts each month, then use that number to figure out the payoff date. You can also use online calculators to see how much interest you'll save by paying your debt early. This last figure can help you stay motivated.

Once you've decided on a monthly amount, and how much of it will go to which debts, add these monthly expenses to your spending plan. You may find after a month or two that you want to adjust your setup. Maybe you shift more money to a different debt. Maybe you increase or decrease your total amount going to debt. It's fine to make changes. In fact, it's good to make changes, because it means you're paying close attention and adapting when you need to. Always remember that this is a journey. The goal is progress, not perfection.

Chapter 33

BUILD YOUR SAFETY NET

You're off to a strong start with your spending plan and your debt payoff plan. Now it's time to plan even further into your future.

You make your spending plan according to what you want your money to get you. That's simple enough in the short term. But you can only see so far into the future, right? There will come a time when you'll want something that isn't even remotely on your radar right now. For example, if I asked you if you wanted a car windshield right this minute, you'd probably be like, "Huh? My car *has* a windshield." But if I asked you after a bird flew into your windshield, leaving a massive crack, you'd probably be all about it, and the faster, the better.

This is where your financial safety net comes in. A financial safety net is exactly what it sounds like. If you have a sudden ER visit, or a broken hot water heater, or a flat tire, your safety net is there to make sure you can cover the cost. It's the resource you can fall back on when the unexpected strikes.

It's also the next step in your money practice. You'll think ahead to what you might want or need in the future, then make a plan to have the resources you need when you need them.

A safety net can have many components, including things like credit access, insurance policies, and estate planning. For now, though, you're going to focus on where you'll apply some of your budget surplus: emergency funds and sinking funds. Emergency funds are a pool of savings set aside for those major, unexpected, out-of-the-blue upheavals. A sinking fund, on the other hand, is a pool of savings for "expected unexpected" expenses, the ones you anticipate spending at some point without knowing exactly when or how much. Although these funds work in slightly different ways, their goal is the same: to minimize risk.

Let's start with your emergency fund. Your emergency fund is there to cover living expenses if you unexpectedly lose your income. That's it. It's there to keep the lights on and food in the fridge. It's a last resort. Before you ever touch your emergency fund, you should do everything you can to cut your spending, scale back your lifestyle, and take advantage of social safety nets. Because once you run out of your emergency fund, you're down to nothing.

This means that some "emergencies" in life are better served by sinking funds or, if those aren't up and running yet, using debt. Say your car dies, and it's cheaper to buy a new car than fix up the old one. Even if you need the car to get to work, that doesn't mean you should tap into your emergency fund. If you drained your e-fund to buy the new car, you wouldn't have cash to cover basic expenses when the job loss hits. So if you have another option to buy the car, such as financing, it's worth exploring, because if anything happens to your income, there's still cash left over for things you can't finance, like groceries and rent.

With that in mind, the size of your emergency fund will depend on the size of what I call your bare-bones budget. Your bare-bones budget is the amount you need to cover one month's basic expenses. You can figure out your bare-bones budget by making a copy of your one-year spending plan, and then removing any costs that you could eliminate or reduce in a crisis. The goal is to have twelve months' worth of bare-bones expenses saved in your emergency fund. But it's fine if you take years to reach that point. A full year's worth of expenses is going to be substantial, after all.

To start, aim for one full month of bare-bones expenses saved in your emergency fund. That will help get you in the habit of building it up. After that, immediately work toward saving three months of expenses as quickly as possible—yes, even at the expense of paying down debt. Remember, your emergency fund is about having that bedrock security. It's the cash you can rely on if you need food, heat, or shelter. Hopefully, it will never come to that, of course. But from this perspective, you can see why it's better to pay a little bit more in interest in order to build up the security of that three-month fund.

To integrate building your safety net into your spending plan, map out target dates and amounts for your one- and three-month emergency funds, and calculate how much you'll need to save each month to hit those targets. Keep your budget surplus in mind as you crunch the numbers to make sure you're staying in range of your spending plan. Then, once you're homed in on a specific monthly savings goal, look back at your spending plan and incorporate that amount into it. After you reach your three-month fund, you can set a longer-term goal to add one, two, three or more months to your emergency fund every year until you hit that twelve-month mark.

The second part of your safety net is those sinking funds. Sinking funds are a way of earmarking cash for expenses that are likely or even guaranteed, but still have a measure of uncertainty. You might know when you'll get a certain bill, but not the amount. You know your dishwasher will tap out *someday*, but not precisely when, or how much a new model will run you.

There are two categories of sinking funds: major and minor. Major sinking funds are for the important things. *Important* doesn't necessarily mean most expensive. It means important to your financial stability. Insurance premiums are a good example. If you can't pay your insurance premiums, you can't pay for your medical care or legally drive your car. Both of those could have significant repercussions on your finances. Similarly, replacing your fridge means dipping into a major sinking fund, because not having a fridge would throw your life out of whack, and probably cost you more in takeout if you couldn't get a new one quickly.

Minor sinking funds, on the other hand, are for nonessential but still meaningful expenses like gifts, vacations, weddings, or saving up for a home purchase. These are things you can live without but you want to be able to have should the occasion arise. Unlike your emergency fund, you might spend from your minor sinking funds a few times a year. If someone invites you to a baby shower, you have a pool for gifts. That's what it's for. But these nonessential purchases are still planned purchases. Your goal is to build solid savings habits, not raid your accounts whenever a small expense pops up. It can be tempting to think that you just need a *little* bit more to cover a cost, so it's okay to tap into savings and put it back when your next paycheck comes in. In the long run, though, it's in your best interest to break that cycle. Instead, I encourage you to look for ways to grow your income and/or cut your expenses.

Once you've identified some ideas for both major and minor sinking funds, you can start to play around with how much you'll contribute each month. Approach this the same way you did the emergency fund, by picking a target date and dividing the total amount into monthly savings goals. Revisit your spending plan and see where your monthly safety net contributions fit in. If your budget surplus accommodates those monthly contributions, you're all set. If not, make tweaks based on your priorities.

The last thing you'll want to decide is where you'll keep your safety net funds. For both emergency funds and sinking funds, you'll want to be able to access that money easily, without delays or fees. So whatever type of account you choose, be sure it allows you to deposit money and withdraw money with minimum (or no) transaction fees, and you're not limited to a certain number of transactions per month (as is the case with some savings accounts). If the account happens to earn you a little bit of added interest on those funds, that's a nice bonus, but you don't need to get too in-the-weeds about the rate. As long as you know where your safety net is and can access it quickly, you're in good shape.

Chapter 34

SIMPLIFY YOUR FINANCES

You've just done a whole lot of strategizing and planning for your money practice. You know what you're doing now and what you want to do tomorrow. Now it's time to look at the operations side of your money practice. How will you get the day-to-day transactions done, and how will you organize them?

The setup I outline below is one way to make your money practice work simply and largely automatically. But it's not the be-all, end-all system. As always, feel free to adapt and change what's here to whatever suits your lifestyle and your preferences.

The one thing I do recommend keeping, no matter what, is the "schedule" step. These check-ins with your spending plan are the best way to stay in tune with it and make it work best for you. But how and when you do those check-ins is completely up to you.

Ready? There are three steps: streamline, automate, and schedule.

STREAMLINE

Streamlining means getting your finances working with the smallest number of moving parts. This means maintaining only as many accounts as you need, having a single system for tracking expenses, and making it easy to check up on your money.

First, you'll examine how many accounts you own: banking, investment, and others. You should have a list of all your assets from your net worth calculation, which should give you a sense of where your money and assets are.

Next, you'll create your simplified system, starting with your checking accounts. You'll want two open checking accounts for this setup. True, two accounts is more than one, but it's all in the name of simplicity, I promise. As you'll see in "Automate" below, the two-account system saves you time and effort by making it easier to spot any shortfalls, so set up those accounts either by consolidating your existing accounts into two or, if you have only one checking account to start with, by opening a second one.

The setup for savings accounts is similar. These are where you'll hold savings for short-term goals and sinking funds and see the total amount at a glance. If your bank lets you open multiple savings accounts with no additional fees, that's a good option. Some banks also have a subaccount or "digital envelope" feature that lets you create dedicated categories within a single account. Either one works here.

When it comes to credit cards, there are additional considerations. For example, it might seem counterintuitive, but you don't necessarily want to close credit card accounts that you're not using. Closing a card removes it from your credit history, which can mean losing a solid track record. If you're in good standing on a card and there's no annual fee, it's fine to keep it to retain the credit history. Stash it in the back of your closet or cut it up so you're not tempted to use it. However, if you have a card with a high annual fee, weigh the pros and cons. You might find that you're fine losing that account from your credit history to save several hundred dollars per year.

Loan consolidation or refinancing might make sense for your streamlining, or it might not. Getting all your loans in one place saves time, but you'll want to weigh that against the new terms of the refi. Read the fine print carefully, and don't feel like you *have* to consolidate just for the sake of making things simple.

It's worth checking up on your investment and retirement accounts as well. If you have retirement accounts from a former employer (or several), look into whether you've been paying fees to maintain them. If so, you might want to research rolling them over to a lower-fee self-managed account.

If you share finances with a partner, streamlining can be a team effort. Sit down and talk about your current money practice as a couple. Are there places it could be simplified? If you rely on IOUs and Venmo to cover shared expenses, it might be worth opening a joint checking account, or adding your partner as an authorized user to your credit card to keep everything in one place. Again, it's all about what makes sense for you.

If you're wondering whether you've left anything out, or if you're just curious, here's an optional bonus step. In the US, each state's treasury department maintains a database of unclaimed property, things like abandoned bank accounts, uncashed insurance payouts, and final paychecks that were never picked up. These databases are free and publicly available to search, so it's easy to look yourself up (be sure you're using your state's official website, which should end in .gov or .us). If you have unclaimed property, your state treasurer or comptroller will help you get ahold of it.

Streamlining Checklist

- ☐ Compile a list of all current open checking and savings accounts, including the amounts held.

- ☐ Review fees (transfer, wire receiving/sending, overdraft, etc.) for all accounts.

- ☐ Review interest rates (if applicable) for all accounts.

☐ Review other requirements (minimum balance, number of monthly direct deposits).

☐ Select two checking accounts to maintain: one for "holding" and one for "expenses." Make sure the bank offers unlimited free transfers and online bill pay (for the next steps).

☐ Set up all income direct deposits to the holding checking account.

☐ Identify short-term savings goals and sinking fund categories, using your one-year spending plan, and create savings accounts (or subaccounts) for each.

☐ Optional: Compile a list of all current credit cards, including account age, balance owed, minimum monthly payment, and annual fees, and assess whether or not to keep each account open.

☐ Optional: Review any existing loans or old employer-sponsored retirement accounts and research refinancing, consolidating, and/ or rolling over the amounts.

AUTOMATE

The next step in simplifying your finances is *automation*. With a little prep work, you can have a system that shows you how much you have for monthly spending, pays your bills, and puts money toward your goals, all automatically.

To start, automate how you monitor your monthly spending. This is where your two checking accounts come into play. First, set up your paycheck (or other income) to be directly deposited to the "holding" account. Then set up a recurring transfer from the holding account to the "expenses" account. Set the transfer amount to be the total you've planned for your monthly expenses.

As you buy things and pay for things over the month, you'll do it from the expenses account. This way, your expenses account serves as a one-stop tracker for how much money you have on hand for the month. You'll be able to see any surplus or shortfall as it starts to take shape. And once you've set it up, it's hands-off. (I do recommend keeping a cash cushion in both the holding and the expenses accounts as a safeguard against overdraft. You'll also want to closely monitor your automation setup for the first few weeks to catch any hiccups.)

For your savings goals, the process is similar. Look at your target monthly amounts to save, either for a goal or in a sinking fund, or to pay toward a debt. Then set up automatic transfers from the holding account to the respective savings accounts.

For bills you pay on a routine basis (monthly, quarterly, or yearly), you'll want to set as many as possible to autopay. Some bills (like utilities, for example) will have online portals to set this up. However, even bills without a built-in electronic payment system can be automated. If your bank offers online bill pay, you can set it up to automatically mail an actual paper check to a specific payee on the schedule of your choosing. This can be a great option for landlords, childcare centers, or any more low-tech payees on your list.

Automating Checklist

- ☐ Find your total monthly expense amount from your one-year spending plan and set up an auto-transfer from your holding account to your expenses account.

- ☐ Use your one-year spending plan to identify your monthly savings and sinking fund goals and set up automatic transfers to the savings accounts.

- ☐ List all your debts, the minimum payments, due dates, and amount you'll be paying under your debt payoff plan.

- ☐ Set debts to autopay the minimum payment every month from your holding account.

- ☐ Set up online bill pay wherever applicable.

- ☐ Optional: Set up monthly automatic minimum payments to credit cards.

SCHEDULE

Of course, there will always be part of your money practice that needs a human touch. After all, your insight and judgment, as well as your personal preferences, goals, and tastes, are at the core of your money practice. Only you can make the decision between, say, a wardrobe refresh this month or a few more days on vacation next month.

That's why the last step in simplifying your finances is to schedule time to review. This is when you grab that cup of tea (or glass of wine), lay out your spending plan, and take a good look. Sit down with your plan and your tracked spending for the month and use the checklist below to get a sense of how you're doing.

When you start, you may want to schedule these reviews more frequently. Monthly, or even weekly, check-ins will help you get the hang of it. Once you feel that your instincts are developing, you can space those check-ins out a bit more.

This setup is for reviewing your spending plan, but you might also choose to recalculate your net worth on a regular basis. Since this recalculation does take time, it's fine to do it quarterly or even semi-annually depending on what fits your schedule. That said, you've already cut out a ton of busywork by streamlining and automating. This means you can spend less time checking totals and crunching numbers and more time making plans for your best life now and your dream life later. And *that* is simply wonderful.

Scheduling Checklist

- ☐ *For the first four weeks:* Block out time on your calendar, add a to-do item, or set a reminder to check in with your simplified setup once a week.

- ☐ Check that:
  - You're covering all mandatory expenses.
  - You're making all needed minimum payments (e.g., on debt) to avoid penalties.
  - You're hitting your savings targets.
  - You generally feel comfortable with your surplus and flexibility for the month.

- ☐ Make any tweaks as needed to ensure all the above points are covered.

- ☐ *After the first four weeks:* Block out time once or twice a month to review finances.

- ☐ If a debt is close to being paid off, stop automatic payments (to avoid overpaying) and schedule the final payment manually.

Chapter 35

PULL IT ALL TOGETHER

I want you to take a quick pause right now. Because you've just done *so* much.

You've looked at your cash flow, net worth, spending plan, debt, and safety net.

You've crunched numbers, played with spreadsheets, and calculated how you'll set off on your journey to live your dream life.

You've taken real action in shaping your life into what you want.

Do you know how amazing that is?

I love understanding money. I love the practice of wealth building. But I also recognize that these things take time and effort. Everything you did in this book, everything you put into building your money practice, asked you to dig deep and think hard. It asked you to define big dreams and core values. It asked for your attention and intention. And you brought it.

So I am thrilled for you right now. In doing all this, you've built new muscles and then flexed them. You made a plan to turn intention into action. You mapped out how to save up for your dreams while *living* the dream. That is—again—amazing.

Now it's up to you to keep it going.

And I promise you—you've got this.

Money is going to be a part of your life for the rest of your life. Money is what's going to make the rest of your life into what it is. But your money practice starts *now*. It's about progress, never perfection.

I chose to call this your money practice because that is what the word *practice* means. A practice isn't a one-and-done checklist or a set-it-and-forget-it system. It's something that needs regular attention and input. But it doesn't ever need to be perfect. It's like practicing the piano, gradually building up your skill with time. Or practicing yoga, going deep on your personal progress and no one else's. Or even like practicing a team sport, finding coaches and communities that can help you push to the next level of possibility.

Most of all, a practice is lifelong. So I want you to take some time and consider how you'll keep your money practice sustainable over the long term.

Sustainable doesn't mean there won't be hiccups. You might stumble. You might have those moments that make you instantly realize you will *not* do that again. But you don't have to let those moments in your journey weigh you down or hold you back. You'll rise above them. You'll know that you didn't fail at anything. You just discovered a good place to tweak your money practice. You learned something and took action with that knowledge.

I know you'll do all this because you already have. Just in reading this book, you've gotten the foundation, the building blocks, and the understanding. You've taken the time to understand and change your money stories. You've started to grow your money capacities. You've defined your dream life. So you absolutely have what it takes to shape your practice over time. Keep up your money practice, and your dream life will become your *real* life.

—— Yes, that's it. All you have to do is keep it up. All you have to do is sustain your practice, and you'll have your best life now and your dream life later.

I hope that idea sounds exciting, because I'm excited for you. I hope you're feeling thrilled and proud and raring to go. But if you're feeling a little nervous, that's normal, too. You're thinking about your *dream life*, after all. That's a big thing to contemplate. But the cool thing is, excitement and nervousness are just two sides of the same emotional coin. You're feeling what you're feeling because your dream life matters to you. All a sustainable money practice takes is to track your progress. Checking in and adjusting. Being thoughtful and in tune with what *you* want. The only thing you have to commit to doing is showing up for yourself. And you've already done that in a big, big way.

There's a short closing statement I say at the end of every session of teaching in Wealth Builders Society. I'll say it to you now: Remember, you deserve to live your dream life, and you have everything you need to make it happen.

I know I might not know you personally (or might not know you yet), but I still know this for a fact.

You've read this book. You've done the work. You've defined what you want from your life. And you know that your money is a tool to make that life happen. And I believe in you.

Now let's take a look at how you can pull all this together.

Action Step

LIVING YOUR MONEY PRACTICE JOURNAL PROMPTS

- Look back at the chapters in part 5 and the actions you took for each. Jot down notes on what you did to set up your practice (knowing your numbers, calculating annual cash flow, etc.) as well as any routine actions you've decided on for the future. Pull it all together and write down a plan, beginning with "My money practice will include the following action steps . . ."

- Now take a step back from the practical side of things. Think about your core goals on the deepest, most value-driven level. What do you stand for in life, and what matters to you as an individual? Journal about how these values show up in your money practice (for example, "I show _____ in my money practice by . . .").

- Brainstorm methods for tracking your progress or sustaining your practice in a way that's easy and enjoyable for you. The more fun (and the more likely you are to do it), the better. Some ideas:

  - A simple tracking chart (on your office wall, stuck to the fridge, in your planner) with an X (or sticker) for every check-in session

  - A jar of something colorful and eye-catching (coins, candies, marbles) that you fill for each X dollars you save/invest/earn in interest

  - A houseplant or fresh bouquet that you associate with your money practice—every time you water (or refresh) it, you'll also sit down to review your spending plan, for example

  - A special ritual for sitting down with your finances: Involve all your senses, using scented candles, chill music, favorite snacks and drinks, and so on

- If you have children, write about how your money practice fits into your parenting philosophy. How is your money practice teaching by example? What are some kid-friendly parts of your money practice in which you can involve the whole family?

- Who can support you in your money practice? Your partner? A friend? An accountability partner? A coach, support network, or program? All of the above?

Acknowledgments

It has always been my dream to write a book, though I thought my first one would be about vampires. That book is still in me, I think. But this one is better. Writing *It's Not About the Money* has been one of the hardest things I've ever done (and I've birthed a ten-pound baby), but I didn't do it alone. The completion of this book would not have been possible without the many individuals who played their part in making this possible. I'd like to thank each of them:

To my literary agents, Jan Baumer and Steve Troha, for being the *best* literary agents a new author could ever want. I am so grateful for your unparalleled determination in pushing this book all the way to the finish line.

To my writing coach, Alexandra Franzen, who dropped everything and helped me mold this book into its current form. Thank you for squeezing me in last minute in between holidays and your vacation. This book wouldn't be what it is today without you.

To my editor, Nina Shield, who provided the perfect balance of invaluable insight and constructive criticism. And to Hannah Steigmeyer, for gracefully handling the unfortunate task of keeping me on schedule.

To my publisher and the entire team at Penguin Random House, I couldn't have done this without you. Thank you so much for your belief in this book and your dedication, patience, and enthusiasm as you helped this new author find her footing.

To my attorney, Marcie Cleary, and the team at Frankfurt Kurnit Klein & Selz PC for handling all the things, because I'm not that kind of lawyer.

Thank you to the friends who have been there to challenge me to show up in the best way, who have helped me grow, and who continue to support me after all these years: Macke and Nicol Maddox, Paul and Allison Rodriguez, and Becca Crootoff and Doug Bernstein.

To Aunt Sharon, Uncle Sherlock, and Aunt Desire, who have always made me feel like I was more than enough.

To Yale Law School, for amazing memories and changing the trajectory of my life forever. I've had the honor of touching millions of lives because you honored me by saying yes all those years ago.

To my children, Alexis and Reeves: Thank you for the love, support, and laughter throughout this process. You inspire me to be the best possible version of myself.

To my amazing husband, Joseph: Thank you for your dad jokes, your unwavering patience, and your steadfast support. You've always encouraged me to follow the random paths I feel called to explore and you've willingly gone on the adventure with me, even though your natural inclination is to put down deep roots and never move. You're quick to remind me that I can do anything. Thank you for being a true partner in this life we share. I love you.

To myself: We've come a long way, my love. I'm proud of you.

And to you, dear reader: This is just the beginning. I can't wait to see where you go from here. Send me a note from time to time and let me know how it's going: scarlett@onebighappylife.com.

Index